THIS HOUSE

First Edition
First published in 2013 by

Woodfield Publishing Ltd
Bognor Regis ~ West Sussex ~ England ~ PO21 5EL
www.woodfieldpublishing.co.uk

ISBN 1-84683-157-1

Last updated 18 November 2013

Front cover illustration: Peter Michael

This House

The remarkable history of a suburban villa in North Ealing, its owners/residents since 1901 and its surrounding square mile in Pitshanger village

RESEARCHED AND WRITTEN BY

JEFFREY PACK

Woodfield

Woodfield Publishing Ltd

Bognor Regis ~ West Sussex ~ England ~ PO21 5EL
tel 01243 821234 ~ **e/m** info@woodfieldpublishing.co.uk

Interesting and informative books on a variety of subjects

For full details of all our published titles, visit our website at

www.woodfieldpublishing.co.uk

The idea for this book came from my wife Jacky
and it is dedicated to her

~ *CONTENTS* ~

Acknowledgements

Many people have helped me with this account and I am grateful to all of them.

Without Jonathan Oates (Archivist at Ealing Library) and his idea of searching the Law Lists for Thomas Richards I would have not found out as much as I did about him. Paul Fitzmaurice loaned me his collection of local pictures, several of which are used here and Andrew Dixon helped with interpretation. David Wallace let me copy his 1777 map of Ealing as well as the original house plans. Geoffrey Nolan helped with the chapter on Ealing golf club; Hugh Mather with the section on St Mary's Perivale; Bruno Callant with the history of St Benedicts; Robin and Ann Oakley helped with their chapter; Derek and Alison of Lyncroft Gardens helped with their history as did Lucy and Bernard and Peter of Queens Walk with theirs and Patrick of Queens Gardens helped with his.

My family helped with their interest and my Editor, daughter Arabella, kept the whole project on an even keel.

Whilst their help has been invaluable the responsibility for omissions, errors and misinterpretations is mine alone.

Jeff Pack
November 2013

Chapter 1: Introduction

The original idea for this book was simply to trace the stories of the people who have lived in 'our' house. The house was built in about 1901 and we have lived here for about 30 years, which is a good chunk of the house's life, but who else has been part of its history? This original idea inevitably widened as the research started and as the house itself developed an identity and almost a personality of its own, separate from its occupiers. It is like an ancient oak tree that has seen wars, Prime Ministers, triumphs and disasters over the years. And thus the book widened to take in, in some detail, the immediate one square mile surroundings of the house, an area the occupiers will have known intimately, to take in also the development of Ealing, but this in fairly general terms, and to take in the social and political life and times over the 100 years or so of the house's life and covering the lives of the occupants. The house started its life with provision for live-in servants and a pony and trap for transport, today it provides for television, washing machines, internet access and central heating.

Any good history should start from the very beginning and that is what I do in the next chapter, which deals with the first 13.7 billion years of the tenth of an acre that the house now stands on. This will bring the story up to more modern times when there is some actual history to record. In the old days this division was referred to as BC and AD. Now it is BCE (Before the Common Era) and CE (Common Era) I like to think the division is between BCE (Before the Coming of Ealing) and ACE (After...)

The one square mile surroundings referred to above are today bounded, for those who know the area, roughly, by Hanger Lane to the east, Uxbridge Road to the south, Western Avenue to the north and Greenford road to the west. For those who don't know the area, the square mile is shown below in 4 maps tracing the development of Ealing. The first map is from 1777, the second 1822, the third from 1876 and the fourth 1914.

Our square mile on the maps is roughly bounded by the Brent River to the north, the two solid parish line markings to east and west and Ealing's Dean to the south, more or less the top half of the 1777 map, and "Our House" is located about half way between the words Pitch-hanger and Hanger Hill on the 1822 map.

The 1777 map is fascinating and I am grateful to David Wallace for allowing me to copy his. The actual map is half as big again as is shown below. The map is surrounded by text, some just visible in the bottom left of the image below. The text is like an inventory of Ealing. The map is dated 1777 with a note that it was revised in 1822. The 1822 map which follows it is clearly different so one assumes the revision was to the text not the map.

The text down the left side of the 1777 map records the dimensions of the parish, the various highways in the parish and whose responsibility it was to maintain them, the renovation of a workhouse with a capacity of 150 people under act of parliament in 1812 (near the New Inn, the pub is still there today) the constitutional status of the parish and its various officers and it notes that "it is perambulated every seven years on Holy Thursday" (i.e. beating the bounds)

Down the right hand side are details of the poor rates (3d in the £ for property owners) as well as census information. In 1820 there were 6,610 inhabitants of the parish. But then comes some delightful detail. "In and about Ealing are many Gentlemen's seats..." and they are then listed.

HRH The Prince of Wales (this was not in 1777, as we shall see, but was in the period up to 1822 and this may apply to others in this list) Princess Amelia, Duke of Marlborough, Duke of Newcastle, Earl Banbury, Earl Weymouth, Lord Clifton, Rt. Hon. Spencer Percival, Bishop of Durham, Bishop of Carlisle, Admiral Sir B Hallowell, Admiral Campbell, Admiral Stephens, General Lord Carnworth, General Sir F Weatherall, General Cameron, General Murray, General Downoviere, Lady Jane Carr, Lady Noel Byron, Lady Stafford, Countess Grosvenor, Lady Glencairn, Lady Seymour, Sir Chas Gould, Sir Thomas Plomer, Sir Thos Edwards, Sir Sampson Wright, Sir Fra Burdett, Sir George Wood, Sir J Wright, Sir John Miles, Col Douglass and Col Morrisson. There is then a list of charities and charitable bequests.

The cartographer of the 1777 map was the Vicar of St Mary's, Ealing, Charles Sturgess, assisted by his churchwardens and the revision was done by a later Vicar, Colston Carr, assisted by his churchwardens. In the list of prominent residents above, they decided to only include titled locals. There must have been just as many untitled but wealthy and eminent locals as well. Ealing then was a very exclusive area.

Although the 1777 map is not easy to read in this condensed form, what is clear is how much empty space there was then and it was predominantly agricultural. The map shows individual properties as well as the names of the owner/occupiers. Given the long list of dignitaries above and the small number of properties on the map, Ealing in the 1777 to 1822 period was clearly a very fashionable area and this is a theme we will return to in a later chapter to find out how this came about. I have shown the map in full and in a more condensed and readable scale.

By the 1822 map Ealing is still a very small hamlet with Brentford, just down the road, considerably bigger and for many years the County town of Middlesex. There has been some development but it is all well south of Ealing's Dean (now the Uxbridge Road) and clustered around St Mary's church. By 1876 the railway had arrived at Ealing Broadway, clearly visible on the map scything through the borough, and urban development had started to creep northwards towards the communications link but still had not started in any meaningful way in our square mile. By 1914 development had crossed the Uxbridge road, as it had by then become, and was filling up North Ealing, and our square mile, and this is the story which we will explore in this book. For the completely up to date picture, just take a look at the A to Z for 2013, there is still a lot of open space but not as much as there was.

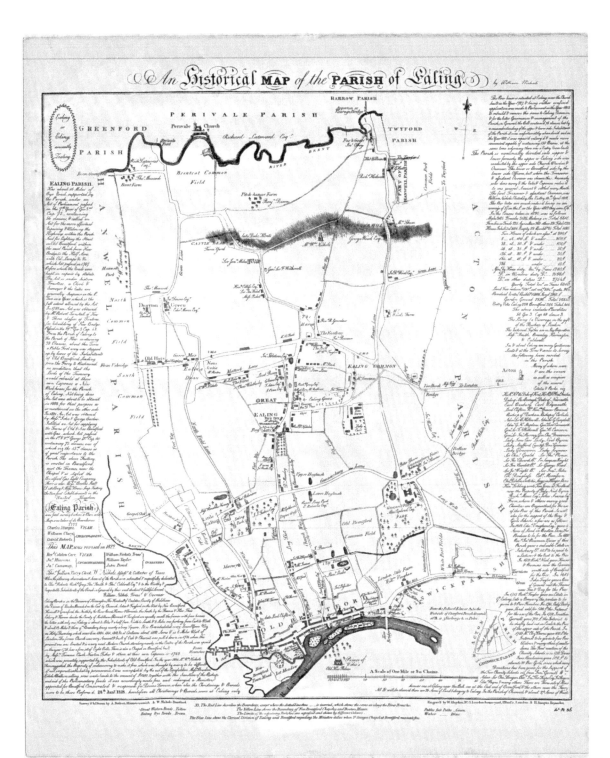

An Historical MAP of the PARISH of Ealing.

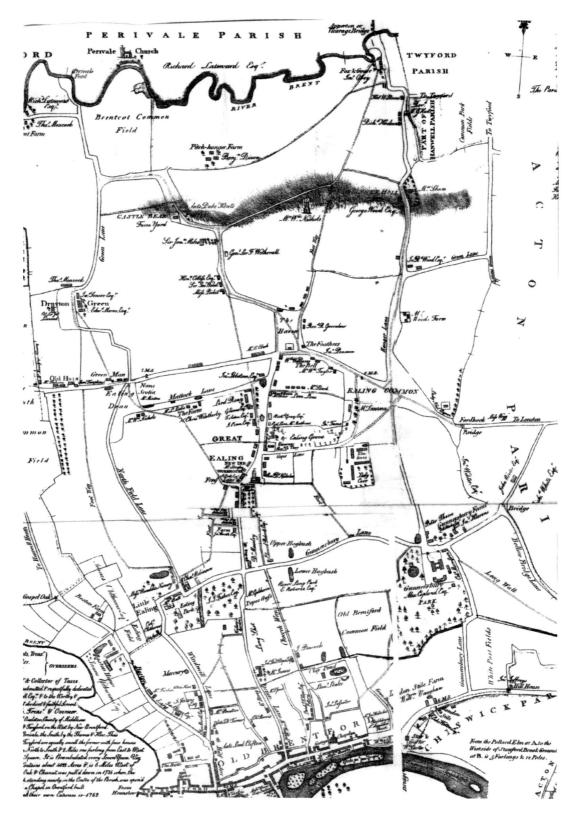

Ealing in 1777

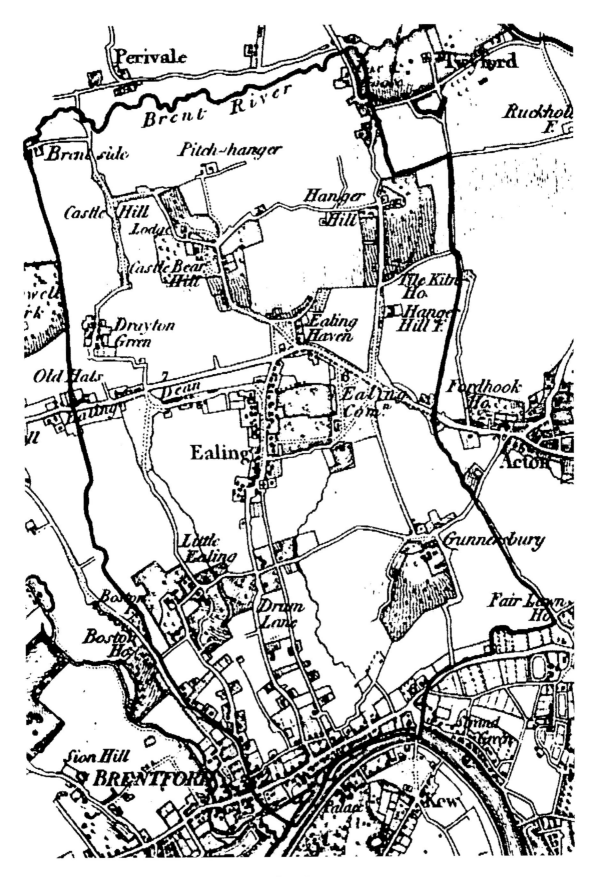

Ealing in 1822

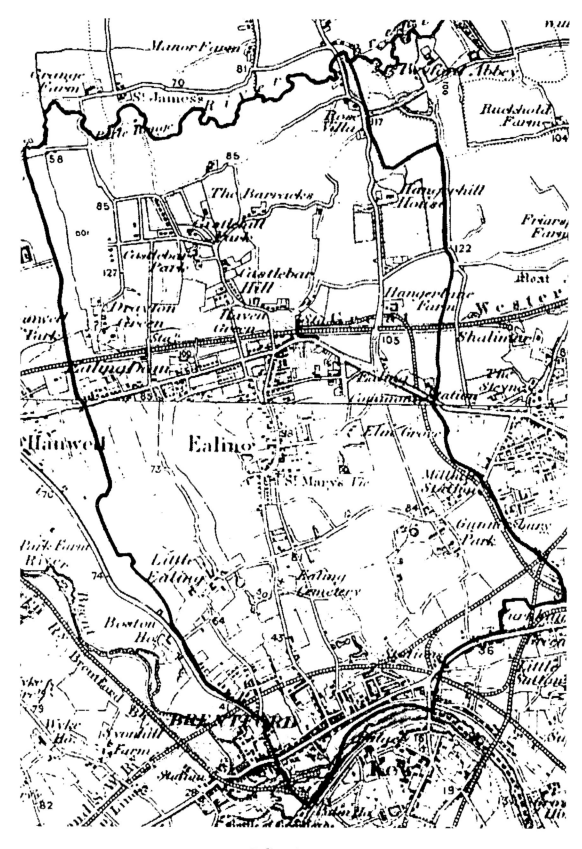

Ealing in 1876

6

Ealing in 1914

Within this area, many interesting things have happened over the years and these will be described in later chapters but for now they may be thought of as Ealing's 3 "R"s – Royalty, Religion and Radicalism.

Chapter 2: In the Beginning

Of course any history of an area must go back to the very beginning but the very early days of Ealing are difficult to chronicle. The Borough first came into being about 13.7 billion years ago when the "Big Bang" created the Universe. But then it was simply a swirling mass of atoms and toxic gasses, there was no atmosphere and no protection against the sun's rays and it was not until about 4.5 billion years ago that the earth was formed. But the earth then was covered by a sea of noxious liquid and it was not until about 300 million years ago that land began to appear in the form of a supercontinent called Pangaea, which comprised all of today's continents. Pangaea is believed to have been located where the Antarctic is now and Ealing would have been located approximately where the Falkland Islands are. As this single land mass broke up and the continental drift created todays land masses Ealing had about 8,000 miles to travel from 51 degrees 41' South, 57 degrees 85' West to today's location of 51 degrees 51' North, 0 degrees 30' West. Extrapolating this direction of travel will see Ealing, in another 300 million years, in the Arctic Ocean, roughly where Novosibirskiye Ostrova is now.

Before Pangaea was formed, life was already beginning; complex multicellular life in the seas existed about 300 million years before Pangaea. This early life would develop and come ashore and gradually evolve into plants, then animals and then, to complete this Darwinian Odyssey, it was about 6 million years ago that the primate lineage developed a strand that eventually led to we humans.

Pangaea 300 million years ago.

The first evidence of humans living in Britain dates from about 800,000 years ago, making them the earliest northern Europeans, but it appears they died out or moved away due to the extreme weather (some things never change) – either rising sea levels or ice-age conditions – and it was only about 12,000 years ago that mankind arrived in Britain for good, making it one of the youngest populations in the world; native Americans, Australians and Africans have inhabited their lands for much longer. There is archaeological Iron Age evidence of occupation in Ealing about 7,000 years ago.

The earliest humans would have been able to come and go quite freely because Britain was still joined to the continent until 300,000 years ago and the Thames flowed into the Rhine and Palaeolithic man first travelled up the Thames looking for Mammoths, Elephants, Hippos, Rhino and Deer. Then, about 9,000 years ago, the Ice Age finally ended, the Ice Sheet melted, the seas rose, Britain became an island and Mesolithic man crossed the North Sea in canoes.

For all of this time mankind had been hunter-gatherers following game wherever it went and not managing the landscape by farming or clearing the forests. And so not very much happened for the next couple of thousand years in Ealing, the hunters chased and ate their game, the forests grew thicker and the Hanger Lane Gyratory System was not on anybody's mind. As we move from BCE to ACE (approximately) this begins to change. But before we move into ACE there was a little bit of bother just down the road.

In 54 BC some rowdy Italian tourists came visiting in the shape of the Roman Empire and Cassivellaunus, King of the Belgae (the Celts) who controlled all of South East England was defeated by the Romans at Brentford, just down the road from Ealing. Under the Romans London became Britain's main commercial port but London then was a long way from Ealing and neither its expansion nor the Romans had much impact on Ealing, life just went on.

In 410 AD, 500 years or so after they had arrived, the Romans abandoned Britain to the Angles and the Saxons and they then began permanent settlements for farming. But again, this had little impact on Ealing. There was little Danish settlement in Middlesex and there still wasn't an Ealing as such, for that we have to wait another 800 years or so and move into the ACE period.

Chapter 3: The Development of Ealing

With the Romans now safely returned to Italy, we are now firmly AD and very nearly ACE. This chapter will cover the next 1,500 years or so until the final dramatic expansion of Ealing and the eventual building of our house and the development of North Ealing.

In the Doomsday Book about 6,000 inhabitants are recorded living in Middlesex in scattered villages. Middlesex (originally Middle Saxon) in those days was far larger than now, stretching all the way to what is now the City of London. A settlement was recorded in the 12th Century roughly where Ealing is now, in the midst of a great forest. The earliest record of habitation was the Putelshanger family in 1222. By the 15th Century Pitshanger Manor Farm extended from Hanger Lane to the Brent. Stags and wild boar roamed the open heath of Hanger Hill.

Ealing's origins were a medieval settlement around Ealing Green, where St Mary's church in South Ealing Road is now. The name became Ealing from about 1700, having been Yelnge, Gillynge, Eling and Zealing in earlier Saxon days. It was entirely south of what is now the Uxbridge Road. The only thing north of the Uxbridge Road, a mile or two away, was Perivale, now part of Ealing. In the Middle Ages the Brent Valley and Horsenden Hill were covered in wheat fields, hay fields and pear trees. By the 16th Century all the forests had been cleared to grow corn for London and Perivale and Greenford became renowned for their wheat fields. Corn buyers flocked to Brentford market, from where the corn was shipped downstream to London and many City merchants bought land in Brentford area. In 1573 Henry Myllet built a moated manor house west of St Mary's church, Perivale and by 1801 there were 28 people living on 5 large hay farms, which provided most of the hay for London's horses. It is interesting that both of Ealing's two early churches chose to be called St Mary's.

Then in the middle of the 17th Century two disasters had an important impact on Ealing. Firstly, in 1665 the Great Plague made London an unsafe place to be if you could afford to move and then a year later in 1666 the Great Fire of London made it even more so. The 10 miles that separated London from Ealing were then all countryside and Ealing must have seemed a safe and convenient place to escape to and many government officials, courtiers and merchants took up residence in Acton and Ealing. By the late 17th Century Ealing had become a fashionable place to live. Henry Fielding (writer of Tom Jones) took a house close to Ealing common, George III spent his summers at Kew Palace and Princess Amelia, daughter of George II, aunt of George III, lived in a mansion at Gunnersbury from 1760 until her death in 1786, when the mansion was pulled down. She had many distinguished visitors; Horace Walpole was a regular. Dukes, Earls, Generals, Bishops, Lawyers and politicians came to Ealing, as we have seen in the 1777 map in chapter one, and by the 19th Century it had developed into one of the most fashionable suburbs of London and had become known as the "Queen of the suburbs". The wayward sons of George III, the Prince Regent and the Duke of Kent, found north Ealing an ideal place to house their mistresses, distant enough from the court at Kew but close enough if they needed money, but more of this later. Ealing Common's most nationally famous resident, Prime Minister Spencer Perceval, has gone down in history as the only Prime Minister to have been assassinated. In 1812 he was shot in the lobby of the House of Commons by a merchant, John Bellingham, who had a grievance against the government. Perceval's daughter, Isabella, married into the profession and is commemorated below in St Mary's church, south Ealing.

In Remembrance
SPENCER HORATIO WALPOLE,
THREE TIMES SECRETARY OF STATE
FOR THE HOME DEPARTMENT
BORN 11TH SEPTR 1806,
DIED AT EALING 22ND MAY 1898.

ISABELLA,
WIFE OF SPENCER HORATIO WALPOLE,
SHE WAS THE DAUGHTER OF
THE RIGHT HON. SPENCER PERCEVAL;
BORN 10TH DECR 1801, MARRIED 6TH OCTR 1835,
DIED 16TH JULY 1886.

Administratively Ealing for a long time was part of Brentford and was dominated by it; indeed Ealing was a very fringe part of Brentford, which was the County town of Middlesex. The reason for this was the importance for the whole area of the Thames and Brentford's docks for commerce and transport, plus, of course, the access for royalty arriving by boat to travel to nearby Kew Palace. It was only in the second half of the 19th Century that this changed and it was the arrival of the railways, and, later still the roads, that was the catalyst, but, again, more of this later. Suffice to say that in a role reversal Brentford is now a fringe part of Ealing. But Brentford will forever eclipse Ealing with its history of famous battles. We saw in the previous chapter that Julius Caesar defeated Cassivellaunus in 54BC in the second Roman invasion of Britain. The next battle of Brentford was 1016 and saw Edmund Ironside defeat the Danes under King Canute, albeit only temporarily. Then the next Battle of Brentford took place in 1642, early in the Civil War, with the Royalists defeating the Parliamentarians only to lose to them several days later in the Battle of Turnham Green. In more recent times battles only occur when local rivals, QPR, play the home team.

And so the development of Ealing began slowly but almost entirely in south Ealing as an offshoot of Brentford. North Ealing remained meadow and farmland for the next 100 years or so and a prominent family there were the Woods.

Richard Wood (1705–83) acquired the lease of 101 acres on Hanger Hill, west of Hanger Lane, to add to existing land holdings, building up a large estate on both sides of Hanger Lane, extending from Acton to Greenford. He and his wife Catherine had 7 children, 3 dying in infancy, and he was succeeded by his second oldest son Thomas Wood. Many of the Woods are buried and commemorated in St Mary's church, south Ealing. The family were the largest property owners in Ealing. Indeed the Wood family must eventually have made a fortune as

Ealing expanded and they eventually sold their land for development. But the Woods did donate land for the building of St Mathew's church, North Common road. By the early 19th Century pastures and enclosed fields had replaced the open fields, and sheep and stock farming were the main occupations in North Ealing. This can be shown in the following Tithe Commutation map of 1839. I have shown this map sideways to make as much detail visible as possible.

A tithe is a biblical term meaning a tenth and was the tax you had to pay the parish for the cost of the rector as well as all the things administered by the parish (and remember from earlier that parishes were about the only day-to-day government in those days) Historically these had been paid in kind, one tenth of your eggs, corn or sheep and this produce was then stored in the tithe barn. The Tithe Commutation Act of 1836 replaced this system with monetary payments and to properly administer all of this parishes were required to produce maps of their jurisdictions with land areas and ownership and the Ealing maps were produced in 1839 and our area is what is shown.

[At this point I hope I will be forgiven a brief aside. For historians it is amazing how much detail and information survives from early days until you realise how much of it is to do with tax gathering by the government or parish, for which records had to be kept. A tangential thought was then prompted by a recently published book that claims that Britain has invaded 90% of the countries of the world at one time or another. The rare uninvaded ones include Guatemala, Luxembourg and Sweden. This inevitably raises the question of whether the British are inherently more warlike than anyone else. I don't know the answer but there is a counter argument that Britain's almost unique history is 1000 years of fairly effective civil governance and therefore 1000 years of tax gathering and therefore of records, and the British have been remarkably compliant in paying their taxes over that time. And of course if a government finds it can fairly readily raise revenue then it will also find that it can amass a war chest. And then finally of course wars are also good for historical records as battalions have to be formed, conscripts sought and so on. It goes without saying that the Tithe Commutation maps were not drawn for the benefit of historians but to increase the tax revenue of parishes]

Turning now to the map, the entire area bordered in blue (amounting to 429 acres) was owned in 1839 by Mrs Mary Ann Armstrong, widow of Henry Armstrong, and was managed for her by Thomas Meacock. (The estate just extends off the top of this map onto the next but virtually all of it is shown.) She died in 1858 and by 1862 the estate was owned by C P Millard (who we will encounter later) The area marked in red was owned by Sir Frederick Augustus Weatherall.

To get some bearings on this map, the farm track marked Scotch Common, which extends to the farm is now Pitshanger Lane and in 1839 it did not extend past the farm. Occupation Road (bottom right) is now Mount Avenue and the red cross is the location of Our House. Running from Occupation Road, close to our house and then down to the farm is a farm track that is now Queens Walk. Green Lane is now Argyle Road.

The fields on the Tithe maps are categorised as to usage and on the map all but two fields are classified as meadows, i.e. for grazing cattle or sheep. The two arable fields are 1508 and 1511. Most of the fields had names as well as numbers. Our House would be built in Target field (16 acres) next to it (1506) was Dog Kennel field. 1501 and 1502 were Lower Wood field and Upper Wood field, both remembered in Woodfield Road today, as is Barnfield Road (1567) immediately behind the farm. Mary Ann Armstrong's holdings would have been entirely commercial. Sir Frederick Augustus Weatherall's holdings will have been partly commercial but probably partly also aesthetic.

We will encounter Sir Frederick Augustus Weatherall in the next chapter and a little bit of background now will not come amiss. He was the Duke of Kent's equerry and Comptroller of his Household. His boss, the Duke of Kent, lived just around the corner. Born in 1755 Weatherall entered the army in 1775 and served in America during the War of Independence. He was Captain of Marines under Rodney at the engagements of Cape Finisterre and St Vincent, was at Gibralter, then Quebec and then the West Indies where he was wounded at the taking of Martinique. Later he served at Madras as a Major-General. He died in 1843. His son, Sir George Weatherall, built Kent House which will feature in the next chapter and the family was very involved with the Duke of Kent; it is said he was visited by Princess Victoria, aged 6, who presented him with a miniature of herself.

Much of the land around these estates was owned by the Wood family, indeed these holdings will originally have been owned by them. The Wood estate was progressively broken up during the 19th century. One factor may have been that their offspring do not appear to have produced any male heirs. Another could be the splitting of their estate by the arrival of the railways at Ealing Broadway, possibly compulsorily purchased, and by then, perhaps, they saw the writing on the wall. The land where "Our House" stands, the square mile shown in the maps in an earlier chapter, was acquired by Charles Millard. He married Frances Ann Claridge and they had 6 children; 4 sons and 2 daughters, so their succession was secured.

And so Ealing expanded from its original centre in South Ealing but scarcely at all, at first, in North Ealing which remained mainly agricultural. One catalyst to change all this was the arrival of Royalty in the early 1800s, the first of Ealing's 3 "R"s and this is the subject of the next chapter.

Chapter 4: Castle Hill Lodge

As we have seen Ealing was already popular with the upper classes but then the ultimate accolade was paid by the arrival of Royalty. And, what's more, just around the corner from "Our House" and comfortably within the square mile radius I have allowed myself.

St David's home is just around the corner from 5 Queens Gardens, about a quarter of a mile away, and is a familiar landmark to all in our part of Ealing. It is now a home for disabled service personnel run by the Sisters of Charity but the site has a remarkable history.

On the present site of St David's Home used to stand Castle Hill Lodge. The Lodge stood in about 30 acres of parkland overlooking the woods and cornfields of the Brent valley and with a fine view towards Harrow on the hill.

Castle Hill Lodge Middlesex
Castle Hill Lodge as it was during the Duke of Kent's tenure, 1801-1819

In 1785 the Prince of Wales, later George IV took Mrs Maria Fitzherbert as his mistress (actually he married her but it was annulled). In 1795 he married Caroline of Brunswick and in the same year leased Castle Hill Lodge and registered it in Maria Fitzherbert's name. Under her occupation the estate grew from a cottage and an orchard to what can be seen in the picture above. For about 6 years a future King of England (from 1820) was a regular visitor to Ealing.

In 1801 the Prince of Wales' younger brother, Edward, Duke of Kent, bought the property from his brother and moved in with his beautiful French mistress, Madame de St Laurent ("Julie"). They lived there for 16 years. Their love story had begun in 1791. They met in Geneva where he was on military studies and she was escaping the French revolution. But there was no prospect of marriage since George III, his father, would not allow marriage to someone non-royal. To try and cure his son of his extravagance as well as his love of a foreign commoner (albeit well born) the King banished Edward first to Gibraltar and then to Alaska but Julie followed him. They returned from Alaska in 1801 and settled down at Castle Hill Lodge. The Duke had very expensive tastes – he employed the architect James Wyatt and gardeners from Kew to create a right royal residence

Here he held dinner parties for friends including his mother, Queen Charlotte, and the future King of France, Louis Philippe. As the 5th child and 4th son of George III Edward must have thought they could stay happily out of the limelight. But their blissful lives in Ealing were to change since there was a bit of a constitutional crisis.

Following the death in November 1817 of the only legitimate grandchild of George III, Princess Charlotte Augusta of Wales, the daughter of the Prince of Wales (she was only 21 and would have become Queen had she survived) the succession began to look uncertain.

As Edward was only the 5th child and 4th son of George III he probably had not expected to be called on to produce an heir but his oldest brother, George IV, lost his daughter (above) and was now estranged from his wife; the second son, Frederick, Duke of York, had produced no issue and was now also estranged; the 3rd son, William IV to be, had no surviving legitimate issue and King George's surviving daughters were all past likely childbearing age, and so the unmarried sons of the King, the Duke of Clarence (William IV to be) the Duke of Kent and the Duke of Cambridge were all encouraged to rapidly contract legal marriages and provide an heir to the throne. Duty called.

With a heavy heart Edward banished Julie (she entered a convent), abandoned Ealing and married Princess Victoria, the widowed daughter of the Duke of Saxe-Coburg, and they produced another Victoria on 24th May 1819 who would eventually become Queen at the age of 18 on 20th June 1837 after the death of her uncle, William IV. She reigned until her death on 22nd January 1901.

Edward, or his courtiers, tried to sell Castle Hill Lodge after he left but it was too expensive and too overdeveloped for anyone's taste and by the time Edward died, in 1820, at Sidmouth, it was still unsold. This was barely a year after he had done his royal duty by producing Victoria; so close did the royal succession come to breaking down.

Edward's executor was General Wetherall and he had to deal with a long line of creditors and, to help matters, he bought Castle Hill Lodge personally. The land of the estate was roughly bounded by Castlebar Hill, Pitshanger Lane, Kent Gardens and Queens Walk.

Later, in 1845, his son, George Wetherall, demolished the old Lodge, sold the contents by auction and built Kent House on the site and much of the surrounding land was bought by Charles Jones, the borough surveyor of Ealing (of whom more later), and divided into building lots. Kent house eventually become St David's Home. Near to Castle Hill Lodge had been The Barracks (which features on some of the earlier maps), there to guard the Royal occupants; these were demolished when Mount Avenue was built in the 1860s.

There have been numerous Royal visits to St David's Home over the years – the Queen Mother, Princess Marina and the Duchess of Kent as well as the Queen herself. How strange for so much recent Royal attention to have been given to a site which 2 of their forbears had used to accommodate their mistresses.

Victoria's reign ended in January 1901. She had reigned for 63 years and 7 months, a record shortly to be overtaken by our present monarch. On 23rd September 1896 there were nationwide celebrations for Victoria's Diamond Jubilee. This was just the time that many of north Ealing's new developments were taking place. It was also a period when Britain's worldwide power was probably at its peak and the popularity of the monarch was also at a peak so it is perhaps not surprising that many of the new roads that were being developed in Ealing, and probably other towns and cities as well, had references to royalty. But this is something one might have expected to find evenly spread around Ealing and for the most part it was not, it was concentrated around the site of Castle Hill Lodge.

Within a short walking distance of the Lodge there are Queens Walk, Queens Gardens, Queens Road, King's Avenue, Prince's Gardens, Kent Gardens, Kent Avenue, Albert Road, Victoria Road, Sovereign Close, Regency Close and Regal Close. The naming of roads is a Council matter and the Borough Surveyor from 1863 until his death in 1913 was Charles Jones and it is very likely that as these new roads were developed he made the link with the history of Castle Hill Lodge, which survives to this day. Thus was our road named.

Following the building of Kent House in 1845, by 1856 it had become the home of an ambitious local architect called Henry de Bruno Austin, of whom more later. It was first established as a residential care home for injured World War One service personnel in 1918 at the instigation of Lady Anne Kerr, daughter of the 14th Duke of Norfolk, and has continued this work ever since. St David's home today is pictured below.

St David's home today

Chapter 5: Recent Times

As we have seen Ealing developed first around St Mary's church in South Ealing and north of the Uxbridge Road, where our house is, was largely undeveloped and this remained the case for most of the 19th Century. One exception was, as we have seen in the previous chapter, Castle Hill Lodge and it will have been the very remoteness of this area that must have appealed to its Royal occupants. Other than this there were a few high class villas dotted about but the area was still mostly farmland.

A major catalyst for change in Ealing was the coming of the railways. In 1838 the Great Western Railway terminus opened at Ealing Broadway; the line was from Paddington to the West Country with stops at Ealing, Hanwell and Southall, amongst others further down the line, and as a result by the 1860s Ealing's population had nearly doubled. Then in 1878 more rail services were started and in 1879 an underground station into London was opened close to the GWR station (it became the District line and was later consolidated into Ealing Broadway station but the original fascia is still there and is pictured below; presumably we have Charles Jones to thank for preserving it although it is now rather lost in the confusion of bus stops and betting shops below.

Ealing Broadway Station.

With these developments an explosion of building took place and the centre of Ealing shifted from St Mary's northwards towards the stations and what had by then become the Uxbridge road. For the next 10 years there was a surge of quality building north of Haven green. Cheaper houses were also built in south and west Ealing but north Ealing, from Castlebar to the Brent

18

and then to Hanger Hill remained almost entirely undeveloped. It was just a bit too far from the station unless you had a pony and trap, which some did, to transport you and it remained mainly pastureland belonging to the Pitshanger estate which had been owned since 1856 by the Millard family.

As Ealing expanded it was fortunate to have a remarkable surveyor to guide and direct this expansion and to make sure it did not get out of hand. Charles Jones (1830 – 1913) was Ealing's first architect, engineer and surveyor. He held these posts for 50 years. He started working for the Council on a commission only basis in 1863 until he was given a salaried post in 1882, which he held until he retired in 1913, shortly before his death in the same year. He had been working into his 83rd year. He made an enormous contribution to the successful and tasteful expansion of Ealing (unlike Acton he would not allow manufacturing in Ealing) during a period when it must have been a bit like the Wild West with developments all over the borough and cowboys and speculators everywhere. He is commemorated by this bust in Walpole Park.

He designed the Town Hall (opened 1888), the Fire Station behind it, Ealing's first proper sewage system, the borough's first Electricity Generating station introducing street lighting in 1894, he acquired Walpole Park (for a mere £40K from Spencer Horatio Walpole, 3 times Home Secretary and Chairman of the GWR) and Lammas Park for public use, he planted the chestnut trees that still adorn Ealing common to this day and much much else.

He also bought much of the land from Castle Hill Lodge for his own private house building projects often in the face of stiff competition; today such conflicts of interest might raise some eyebrows. We saw above that he had worked on a commission only basis until 1882 when he was given a salaried post. He may well have been put on the payroll to prevent such conflicts of interest. Perhaps the Council concluded that a poacher turned gamekeeper was best placed to control the tearaway expansion of the town. This he certainly did but above all he maintained the quality and standards of that expansion. There was almost certainly no standard Council design for new housing projects but it may well have become clear what sort of proposals would be approved both as to house design but also sizes of houses, density of housing, street names and so on. Charles Jones insisted that all new roads had to be kerbed, channelled and finished with flint before houses could be erected, all this at the developers expense.

Developers came in all shapes and sizes, some small scale, some very large, sometimes private individuals, sometimes building societies. One early attempt at a large scale housing scheme was by Henry de Bruno Austin. His plan had been for a 190 acre Castle Hill estate of middle class villas. In the event he actually built just 20 or so semidetached houses in Kent Gardens and Cleveland Road between 1863 and 1867, all of which are now gone, before becoming bankrupt in 1872. There are several interesting aspects to this story. Firstly it is clear that property development was not a guaranteed money spinner. Secondly, this was the first attempt to develop north Ealing in a serious way. It failed but 30 years or so later, as we shall see in the next chapter, others succeeded but in an entirely different way. Henry de Bruno Austin's plan is shown below. To get some bearings St Stephens's church is in the centre foreground and Kent Gardens is at the extreme right.

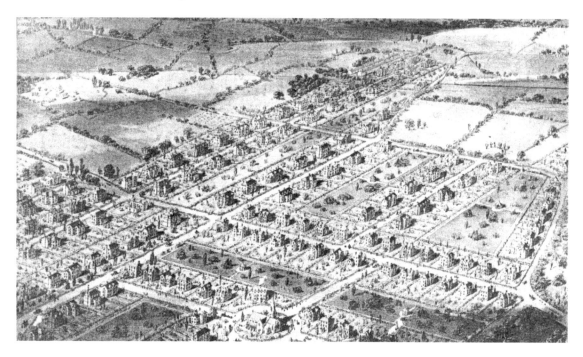

There was another aspect. When we came to buy our house in 1982 the solicitors found that a charge had been registered against the property, namely, "A conveyance dated 16th November1865 between Charles Paul Millard (the landowner then) and Henry De Bruno Austin" which contained restrictive covenants. It did not take long for the solicitors to establish that this was no longer effective. But one has to assume that this was some sort of call option taken out by Austin with a view to an eventual purchase and perhaps he had taken such options all over the area and his eventual bankruptcy was simply because he had over extended himself in his rush to build. Charles Jones will undoubtedly have known Henry de Bruno Austin (who lived in Kent House, the successor to Castle Hill Lodge, until his bankruptcy), maybe they did deals together until Jones went on the staff?

After Henry de Bruno Austin's failed attempt at large-scale development of north Ealing things quietened down for a while. Following the railways, houses began to appear on the north side of Haven green but the gentlemen's residences on the hill were still undisturbed. Everywhere else in Ealing was a hive of activity but the hillside was still farmland. Pitshanger farmhouse was located in Pitshanger lane where it meets Queens Walk, and both these roads were simple farm tracks then. Pitshanger farmhouse was only finally demolished in 1908 and is pictured below shortly before its demolition; the new Brentham houses in Barnfield Road can be seen in the background and the old farmhouse would soon be surrounded by new development. In the picture it looks deserted and the sign in the garden is probably "For sale"

And so Ealing, from having been a small medieval settlement around St Mary's in south Ealing for a thousand or so years and having then expanded into central Ealing with the coming of the railways from the 1850s onwards was finally ready to make its last expansion into north Ealing, after one failed attempt 30 years earlier, and the start of that development is the subject of the next chapter.

Chapter 6: The Brentham Garden Suburb

At the same time as the capitalist feeding frenzy was going on elsewhere in Ealing (and would start soon in Queens's Gardens) an almost unique socialist experiment was taking place comfortably within our square mile, in fact just down the road; one wonders what the Duke of Kent would have made of it? In fact, as we shall see, his grandson opened the social club in 1911.

The catalyst for the experiment was Henry Harvey Vivian, 1868-1930. He was born in Devon and moved to London at the age of 18 seeking work as a carpenter. He was also very involved with trade unionism and the Labour Association and politics in general and was elected to Parliament as the Lib-Lab MP for Birkenhead in 1906 and then the Liberal MP for South Somerset in 1911 and then variously in and out of Parliament at Edmonton, Northampton and Totnes. He was described as a "practical mystic" and he espoused the concept of Co-partnership for housing development (this is the second of Ealing's three "R"s – Radicalism). In 1901 (aged 33) he formed a small group to develop the idea which included Hubert Brampton whose father was landlord of the Haven Arms and it was at the Haven Arms (which is still there) that they had their early meetings. They were a mixed group of Fabians, Socialists, Atheists and Liberals but what united them was a desire for affordable housing for workers in which they would have an active interest, in other words not council housing. All the housing development elsewhere in Ealing was completely unaffordable to workers. Their objective was "to provide for the pastimes and pleasures of people within sight of their own homes; and, by a well ordered disposition of land give a family in a small house all the natural advantages of landscape and garden outlook hitherto only possible to a man with large possessions"

Henry Vivian must have been an incredibly dynamic man. He lived in Burgoyne Road, Haringey, north London, quite a distance from Ealing. He had the parliamentary responsibilities noted above, he took a keen interest in housing developments elsewhere in England as well as overseas, as we shall see below, and he owned his own building company, General Builders Ltd (thus his interest in Co-partnerships was both philanthropic, practical and probably highly profitable since his company did most, if not all, of the building of the Brentham estate) He is pictured opposite, second from the left, at a conference in New York in 1913, and he would appear to be mixing with toffs.

The business model for Co-partnership was that a company, Ealing Tenants Ltd, would be set up which would invite applications for shares, subject to a maximum, so no-one could dominate, and a minimum, so all contributed, and this, together with the issue of loan stock, would allow the land to be bought by the company and the houses to be built, and in the fullness of time ownership of the society would transfer from outside investors, as the loan stock was repaid, to the tenant shareholders. You would never actually own <u>your</u> house; you would instead be a co-owner of <u>your</u> estate. "What we want is wholesale economy and retail responsibility" i.e. all tenants should have a healthy self-interest coupled with a commitment to collective ideals. It was hoped that the absence of individual ownership would encourage strong community spirit. The company paid 5% to shareholders and 4 ½ % on its loan stock. Tenants would get fair rentals and shareholder tenants would have their 5% credited to them as accumulated shares, thus increasing their stake in the estate. The idea was that this structure would secure continuity of interest and goodwill on the part of the residents. The concept and the company had many influential supporters including Leopold de Rothschild.

There are still signs on some houses from those days,
this one is in Woodfield Crescent

The first group that got together as shareholders to develop Brentham were genuine workers and craftsmen – plasterers, painters, carpenters, an engraver, a Police Constable, a valet and a schoolmaster amongst others. The Millards (Charles Anthony and his son Edward), the owners of the land which would be leased to Ealing Tenants Ltd, were also involved.

The company moved quickly, several months after their first meetings in the Haven Arms, acquiring land in Woodfield Road (previously the Lower Wood field of the farm, the Wood family having been the original owners of the land until the Millards bought them out) Building began on 20th April 1901 at what is now 71-87 Woodfield Road, for a while known as Vivian Terrace, and the first house was occupied on 12th April 1902. As we shall see later this was probably at almost exactly the same time as 5 Queens Gardens was finished and occupied, indeed the occupiers of both houses would probably have been able to see each other, there having been nothing but fields in between them. Is it possible that Albert Boehr, who we will meet later, and the Woodfield occupier knew each other and discussed the relative merits of capitalist and cooperative housing development at a local pub?

Some of the early Woodfield houses were bought by Charles Millard as investments; this was probably allowed to help the company's cash flow but would seem to have been an early departure from the original ideals, the first of other departures to come as we shall see.

Between 1903 and 1910 membership of Ealing Tenants Ltd rose from 59 to 353; share capital from £1,442 to £25,600, loan stock from £2,366 to £35,700; and the value of property from £10,237 to £158,000. Rents ranged from 6s. 6d. to 21s. per week, exclusive; it being a principle of the co-partnership philosophy that payment of rates and taxes by tenants would encourage a sense of civic responsibility. All dwellings were equipped with baths, though not all had bathrooms; in the flats the bath was placed in the kitchen. It was stipulated that gardens must be divided only by hedges. Five acres of the estate was reserved for allotments, and twelve acres for playing fields.

Today the estate is 600 houses and 70 flats on 50 acres. It was almost all built by 1915 when it was still largely surrounded by open land. The First World War brought everything to a stop as the cost of materials soared and building workers were enlisted, and expansion after the war was never resumed. The population of the estate in 1915 was 2000 but by then it was predominantly clerical and professional which was never the original intention. The original plan had been for 100 houses but it just kept growing and growing.

In good socialist fashion the estate would have a social centre, the Brentham Institute, now the Brentham club. This was built in 1911 and opened on 27th May of that year but was not licensed, indeed no licensed premises were allowed on the entire estate. The original plans for the Institute were for something much larger, 3 times as big, with a men's hostel, bachelor flats and more but these were never completed. The Institute provided accommodation, a concert hall, reading room, Ladies room, billiards tables and so on; it was for indoor sport (it was only much later that the outdoor sports facilities were added) and worthy things, lectures on abstinence and Fabianism, self-improvement, and debating. It was officially opened by Queen Victoria's youngest son, Prince Arthur, the Duke of Connaught, thereby continuing the family's interest in the area. The Brentham club is pictured today below; it became a private sports club in 1947.

During the period that the Brentham estate was being built, co-partnership housing had become a national movement. The Co-partnership Tenants Housing Council had been set up in 1905 to advise numerous other societies, and a federation of tenants' societies had been established, known as Co-partnership Tenants Ltd, under the chairmanship of Henry Vivian. His advice on Co-partnership housing schemes was eagerly sought, with the result that many of the later Co-partnership schemes closely followed the ideas of Ealing Tenants and the Brentham estate. At Letchworth, Garden City Tenants Ltd had close associations with Brentham, and at Hampstead Vivian organised a tenants' society on the same lines as Ealing Tenants. The movement also spread overseas to many countries, including Germany, Canada and Russia. Vivian remained chairman of Ealing Tenants until 1911, when he resigned in favour of the vice-chairman, William Hutchings. His achievement was summed up by the journal *Co-partnership* (January 1912) in the following comment: 'In the whole history of Industrial & Provident Societies during the last sixty years there is probably no instance of greater results from such small resources than in the case of Ealing Tenants Ltd. whose leadership Mr Vivian has now relinquished.'

But there were rumblings of discontent on the estate from quite early on. There was unease as the estate got bigger than had been originally planned, there was a feeling that Ealing Tenants Ltd was not serving the tenant's purposes and was more interested in developments elsewhere and was almost becoming capitalist in outlook. There had been discontent from very early about the sizes of the houses and reconciling the need for them to be small and affordable for workers but still sufficiently large and profitable to satisfy the holders of the loan stock as well as the freeholders, the Millards, who wanted security of their rent. As a result of this tenants were increasingly not the tradesmen foreseen and there was a gradual incursion of the middle classes and as early as 1906 there were 2 clergymen, 6 schoolmasters, civil servants and chemists, not the population originally foreseen.

Another factor may have encouraged this middle class influx. The Brentham estate, indeed most of north Ealing, was one of the last parts of Ealing to be developed because of the distance from the stations. For workers, perhaps with toolkits and materials to carry and working in different places all the time, this would be a disincentive. For teachers, civil servants and clergymen, with only a briefcase to carry and perhaps working locally this would be less of a problem. This may also explain why the Millards agreed to allow the Brentham estate to be built. Surely they would have preferred the more profitable (to them) capitalist approach? Perhaps they thought that Henry Vivian and his Co-partnership was their last chance to do something with this land?

For Henry Vivian the attraction of Brentham may well have been that the land was cheap and it was cheap because it was so far away from any facilities. A related factor perhaps encouraging the eventual worker exodus was that the first tenants were almost certainly the workers who built the estate (working for Henry Vivian) and it was when the estate was finished in 1915 that this communications issue arose. For some it may have been an issue even earlier. When the estate design went Arts and Crafts in 1906 it may be that some workers found they did not have the necessary skills for this new type of building.

One original principle had been that all tenants would be shareholders and all shareholders would be tenants, thus ensuring a common interest. It did not take long for this to break down. The estate accepted tenants who could not afford to be shareholders and there were shareholders who were not tenants. One famous example was George Bernard Shaw. He had roundly criticised the Co-partnership concept, it was not left wing enough for him, but he still invested large sums in the enterprise and was one of its largest shareholders.

As the original principals were mainly atheists another original tenet had been that there would be no church on the estate. But St Barnabas Church was built in 1916 and is pictured below. The original principals were also strong advocates of temperance but in 1935 the Brentham Club got a license to sell alcohol.

By the 1930s Ealing Tenants Ltd began selling off their houses to resident tenants, initially on 99 year leases but, after 1931, freehold. By 1968 around two thirds of the suburb was privately owned and today there are just a few properties left that are rented (from Bradford Property Trust Ltd which is where Ealing Tenants Ltd ended up when it was dissolved)

When building first started on the Brentham estate the residents were regarded as a lefty commune of sandal wearing allotment gardeners, they were all cranks and subversives. It did not take long for the middle classes to overwhelm these ideals.

The first houses that were built on the estate were the "Woodfields" (Road, Avenue and Crescent) between 1901 and 1906 and these are fairly standard Edwardian terraced houses and they don't seem to have had an architect, just a standard contractor design. Examples are shown below.

The first houses built in what is now Woodfield road were called Vivian terrace in honour of their developer and the terrace is shown below (did Charles Jones insist on a more conventional road name?)

But in 1906 this all changed with the appointment of F. Cavendish Pearson as architect, to be succeeded by G.L. Sutcliffe in 1910 until 1915 and under these two architects all new houses were built in the Arts and Crafts design and examples are shown below to compare with those above. Was this perhaps further evidence of the drift towards satisfying the middle classes?

The Arts and Crafts design movement flourished between 1860 and the first World War and was inspired by William Morris, John Ruskin, Augustus Pugin, Edwin Lutyens, Charles Voysey and many others and it was a sort of Gothic revivalist movement that stood for traditional craftsmanship using simple forms and often using romantic or folk styles of decoration as applied to paintings, crockery, craftwork and much else as well as buildings. This would seem a very middle class design to apply to what were supposed to be workers cottages. Is it possible that even by 1906, just 4 years after it started, that middle class tastes were directing the development of the Brentham estate?

Whilst it is pure conjecture on my part it is tempting to compare Henry de Bruno Austin and Henry Harvey Vivian and to perhaps conclude that they both failed. Austin, the capitalist entrepreneur, definitely failed by becoming bankrupt and actually building only a handful of houses. His scheme probably was simply too large; the original plan was for an estate four times the size that the Brentham estate ended up at. Vivian failed because his ideal was for a workers cooperative housing development and this was not realised. Indeed perhaps his resignation from Ealing Tenants Ltd, noted above, in 1911, is evidence of this disillusionment. One would have thought that by 1911 most of the estate was built and most of the problems should have been over and now would have been the time to settle back in his chairmanship and enjoy the reflected glory. The original Co-partnership group may have failed in many of their lofty utopian ideals but they did nonetheless leave a legacy of beautiful buildings as shown below.

Although Vivian terrace is now Woodfield road not all trace of Henry Vivian is lost. Opposite the Brentham club is a small area called Vivian green and it is pictured below and it has been recently commemorated.

Vivian green

My parents lived in Fowlers Walk, on the estate, for about 10 years. So also did Fred Perry (1909 – 1995) 3 times Wimbledon champion; his family arrived in Brentham in 1918 and they moved into 223 Pitshanger lane. His <u>first</u> game of tennis was at the Brentham club ("Institute") at the age of 15. Other sporting heroes were Mike Brearley, England cricket captain who started his cricket career at the Brentham club and Peter Crouch who began his football career there.

There is an active preservation society to protect this amazing and almost unique garden suburb from unsightly extensions, inappropriate new windows and ugly aerials and so today the estate is almost unchanged from when it was built more than 100 years ago, as the following pictures attest.

At about the same time as the Brentham suburb started another definitely middle class development occurred close by, Ealing golf club. This would have served the Dukes and Generals and not, until recent times, the tradesmen, and this is the subject of the next chapter.

Chapter 7: Ealing Golf Club

I am grateful to Geoffrey Nolan, a friend and fellow member of Ealing Golf club, for most of the content of this chapter.

A sure sign of gentrification is the arrival of golf clubs and north Ealing, with its Dukes and Generals, was no exception.

Ealing golf club was founded in March 1898. Its original name had been the Castlebar Golf Club after Castle Bear farm, roughly where Notting Hill School is now. There had been two previous attempts to form a golf club, both at Twyford Abbey, now the Guinness brewery and Park Royal estate, firstly in May 1891 and then again in 1894, but both failed over issues of land tenure. It is quite likely that this site for the golf club was successful because it could not be developed, surrounding as it does, the river Brent and for the most part being a flood plain.

The club was founded by three local dignitaries – Messrs Gibbon, George and Way. Alfred A. George was an antiquarian and has given his name to a cup, which is still competed for to this day. Henry Gibbon was a local property owner who lived in Kent House after Henry de Bruno Austin's bankruptcy; he was clearly a wealthy man, since he bid successfully for about 20 of the 153 lots which were auctioned in May 1881 of a part of the Castle Hill estate which became Castlebar Park Road. About Mr Way, nothing is known.

The first clubhouse, which was opened in 1898, was in two large semi-detached Victorian houses at the bottom of Kent Gardens on the west side. These were two of Henry de Bruno Austin's houses. They contained bedrooms for the use of members, a handsome smoking lounge, billiards and card rooms, and a tennis court in the garden. From this clubhouse the 1st and 18th holes were across Scotch common. The house was demolished in the 1960s to make way for the Clevelands estate. In 1905 the club lost Scotch common and now the clubhouse was a long way from the rest of the course. The course had to be changed for this and a new clubhouse was built behind what is now the 6th green. The club President at the beginning of World War 2 was Mr Leopold de Rothschild who lived in what is now Gunnersbury Museum.

With the opening of the Western Avenue in 1931, the club lost yet more land and had to be redesigned again. This meant that, yet again, the clubhouse was in the wrong place and in April 1930 it was built in its current location.

In World War 2 more land was lost (albeit temporarily) when an anti-aircraft gun site was installed to help defend the Hoover building, which was making aircraft parts. There was also a military firing range shooting from where St Benedict's playing fields are now to the club's 6th tee. This is marked on 19th century maps and the area by the 6th tee remains one where grass does not grow successfully, possibly due to the lead contamination.

One notable member was Harry Beckham Randolph, who joined the club in 1920, aged 23. He was Chairman of the club from 1935 to 1971, when he moved to Dorset and bought the Isle of Purbeck Golf Club. He was also Chairman and Managing Director of Wilkinson Sword from 1935 to 1966, and then President until 1971.

Golf undoubtedly was a snobbish, middle class and essentially male sport years ago. Today that has all changed and it is as inclusive as any other sport. But when Ealing golf club was founded in 1898 it will definitely have been intended solely for the grandees of north Ealing and certainly not for the tradesmen of the Brentham estate. Evidence of this comes from a minute of the Club's 1919 Annual Meeting:

"The Captain intimated that as several Ealing tradesman were desirous of joining the Club it might be desirable that the matter be discussed by the members present. This, after some discussion, was not considered desirable, and the matter was dropped. The Meeting considered that this was solely in the province of the Committee."

Chapter 8: Churches

This is the last chapter describing the surroundings of Queens Gardens and the background and history of the area. After this, we concentrate solely on our house and its residents. This chapter will be on the last of the Ealing 3 "R"s. The first was **R**oyalty and Castle Hill Lodge. The second was **R**adicalism and the Brentham estate. This chapter is **R**eligion and churches.

The first church has already been mentioned; St Barnabas was built in 1916, barely a dozen years after the starting of the atheist, left wing suburb of the Brentham garden estate with its resolve to have no churches. Henry Vivian resigned as Chairman of Ealing tenants Ltd in 1911; was this when the planning for the church was beginning with its final abandonment of yet another of the fundamental principles?

There are three other churches to mention. The reason they are important to our story is because churches held a very different position in everyday life then than they do now. As well as providing spiritual guidance and community support they were where the parish council met and deliberated. Until the 20th century, central government and its agencies played very little part in people's lives. Parish councils played a big part. They were, in effect, the Police, DHSS, operators of the Poor Laws, Taxation authority and much else. That is why communities sprang up around churches and the three we will briefly cover are St Mary's, south Ealing, St Mary's, Perivale and St Benedict's; two Anglican churches and one Roman Catholic.

St Mary's in south Ealing was at the centre of the original settlement of Ealing and dates from the early 12th Century (it is recorded as being operational in 1127). For many years it was the only church in a huge area stretching from the Thames at Brentford north towards Wembley, west

beyond Southall and east to Acton and Bedford Park. At the end of the 16th Century there were only 427 inhabitants in this whole area. In 1698 the church founded Great Ealing School, reputed to have been the "finest private school in England" with famous pupils such as William S. Gilbert and Cardinal Newman. The school is now gone as is the original medieval church and much of its Georgian replacement and today's church, pictured below, was consecrated in May 1866, just at the time that the centre of gravity of Ealing was moving northwards. The architect was Samuel Sanders Teulon who specialised in Gothic revival churches. The new church was consecrated by Bishop Tait who commented that St Marys had been transformed from a Georgian monstrosity into a Constantinopolitan Basilica, a Byzantine shrine. The outside of the church is fairly austere but the inside, especially after the renovation work done in 2003, is stunning.

And now to St Mary's namesake in Perivale.

St Mary's, Perivale, dates back to 1135 and was the church for the hamlet of Perivale which in 1881 had only 34 residents and until the 1920s comprised only 5 farms. It had served this tiny community for 800 years, perhaps more since it was probably built on the site of a Saxon predecessor. For all this time Perivale had been separated from Ealing by the river Brent. The Brent is too shallow and winding to be navigable or to provide power and the regular flooding meant little was ever built near it but it was a barrier not easily crossed and Perivale remained very quiet and solitary for centuries comprising just a manor house (demolished, or collapsed, about 1784) the church, its rectory and the farms.

Then, poor Perivale, around 1930, the Western Avenue (A40) was built and sliced right between the church and its community, which by 1950 had grown to 10,000. A new church north of the Western Avenue was built in 1965 and St Mary's became redundant, and stranded, until rescued by volunteers who turned it into music and arts centre. Today, it stands proudly right in the middle of Ealing golf club, between the 9th tee and the 12th tee, to the great mutual benefit of both. The banks of the river Brent are just visible in the foreground.

St Mary's, Perivale

But there is an interesting twist to the story of St Mary's. The graveyard is full of people who have nothing whatsoever to do with Perivale. In the 18th and 19th centuries it became common, almost fashionable, for the wealthier inhabitants of London to bury their deceased relations in a quiet, leafy, country resting place well away from the bustle and grime of central London and so personalities with no connection with the district were being buried there. In the early 19th century there was an added reason for avoiding burials in central London. The corpses of executed criminals were the only legal source of bodies to teach surgeons anatomy and there was a shortage of them and so grave robbing became a lucrative business and so if you wanted to prevent your deceased relative ending up being dissected in St Thomas' hospital you found somewhere safe like Perivale. This went on until 1906 when the People's Warden, Mr Louis Roberts, took legal action against the then Rector, who had made a lot of money from selling the plots, to stop this; by 1884 the graveyard had had to be extended such was the popularity of this practice; of the 416 burials between 1813 and 1900 less than one eighth were of local parishioners.

Amongst the non-locals are Robert Cromwell of Paddington, died 1722, a probable relation of Oliver, Admiral Sir Richard Collinson, 1811-1863, arctic explorer of the north west passage and first explorer to survey parts of the east coast of China and Admiral Carter who fought at the battle of Trafalgar. The picture of the graveyard below is self-evidently not that of a poor rural agricultural parish, with all the memorials and stonework.

40

The Rector in question was Charles Hughes, born in 1838 and Rector from 1861 until his death in 1907. He was an educated man with an MA in 1855 from Cambridge and St Mary's must have been almost his first and only job. In 1882 he wrote a letter to the Times presumably in response to someone else's letter:

"*A parish in Wales with only 21 inhabitants and 620 acres in extent is hardly so peculiar as a parish 7 miles from the Marble Arch, with only 34 inhabitants and 626 acres in extent. The parish of Perivale, 2 miles from Ealing, fulfils these conditions (there are in all 5 houses), being the smallest parish in the diocese of London, and one of the smallest in England*" It was reported that "*at a vestry meeting 3 years earlier to authorise the sale of the organ, no one but the Rector attended and he had, not for the first time, to propose and second the resolution and declare it carried. As was his usual practice, he then proposed a vote of thanks to himself and declared the meeting closed. In 1901 only 2 parishioners attended a meeting held for the same purpose.*"

And at a meeting held for the appointment of an overseer, a Mr Smith objected to Hughes' appointment on the grounds that he held all the other parish offices. With all this unfettered power it is perhaps not surprising that he misused it for "unofficial" burials that benefited him personally. Charles Hughes is pictured below.

Rector Charles Hughes.

Until 1885 he lived at Castlebar Court (later University College hall) in Queens Walk, next to the Duke of Kent's estate and pictured below. Then he sold the property and moved into the Perivale Rectory. Castlebar Court was destroyed by bombs in the war (this is barely 300 yards from our house) and the Perivale rectory was demolished in 1958.

Charles Hughes must have been almost unique in the Church in living in a property that appears to be at least ten times the size of the church where he worked. He must also have been a wealthy man. He is likely to have been the 3rd or 4th son of a prosperous family wherein the first son traditionally went into the army, the second into the diplomatic service and later ones into the church or schooling. He was clearly not very ambitious staying in such a small parish all his life with presumably minimal parish earnings and few parishioners to minister to. University College hall appears to have been a language school for French and German students. Did he sell it because his graveyard business occupied too much of his time and was considerably more profitable?

All that remains of University College Hall, after it's bombing, is one of the entranceways, pictured below. The post war flats behind are now Dene Court.

The question of the popularity of the churchyard for burial became especially important at the turn of the century as there was an awakening of interest in the church and the good of the parish. At a vestry meeting held on 24th May 1906 the chairman 'objected to the appointment of

Mr G Valentin as churchwarden as he was a non-parishioner and not a house-holder' A large number of people from Ealing interrupted the proceedings at this point and the meeting was adjourned *'as it was impossible to proceed amidst such tumult'* Having seen how small the parish was it is not clear where all these people came from or who they were. Charles Hughes was apparently High Church bordering on Anglo Catholic becoming more so in later life. Is it possible they were atheists from the rapidly expanding Brentham estate or possibly, given the developing Catholic presence at St Benedict's (next church) were anti-Catholics? When the meeting was resumed *"the question of the burial of non-residents was raised as the People's warden, L Roberts, explained be objected to the burial of non-parishioners because ...'there was little room left in the churchyard and new ground would soon be required"'* Legal action was taken by Mr Roberts against the rector Rev Hughes, to prevent continuance of the practice, and it was successful, and the internment of non-parishioners ceased with the exception of those who had family graves and vaults. Charles Hughes died barely a year later. I am grateful for the above pictures of Charles Hughes and his house and some of the details about him to Hugh Mather, chairman of the Friends of St Mary's.

The church also has a lych gate pictured below. "Lych" is the Saxon for a corpse and the lych gate was where the clergy met the corpse and the bier rested before burial. It is believed that St Mary's lych gate was built in 1904. Perhaps Rector Hughes built this to further embellish the church so as to continue attracting noble fee-paying interments and perhaps this was the final straw that led to the legal action above in 1906? It is puzzling because the graveyard must have been almost full in 1904? The picture below was taken in 1920 and the lych gate is still there.

Also within our square mile is the Catholic church of St Benedict's, now Ealing Abbey, a Benedictine monastery. The Benedictines bought 2 acres of the Castle Hill House estate in 1897 to found the first Benedictine Abbey in London since the Reformation. The Abbey itself was built in 1899 (and rebuilt in the 1960s) and occupied by Benedictine monks from Downside Abbey. The school associated with the Abbey was opened in 1902 and has had numerous famous alumni including Peter Ackroyd, Julian Clary, Chris Patten, Denis MacShane and Labi Siffre.

Originally, in 1897, St Benedicts was only a monastery (as a monastery the site must have seemed perfect, on the side of a hill, secluded and surrounded by countryside, ideal for contemplation, it did not remain secluded for very long); it became a Priory in 1916 and then an Abbey in 1955. In the immediate area around the church are a large number of Catholic orders; the Brothers of St Gabriel, the Capitanio Sisters at Nile Lodge, just round the corner from Our House in Queens Walk, the Domenican Sisters, the Little Company of Mary, the Marian Fathers (a Polish order), the Missing Sisters of our Lady of Africa, the Sisters of Charity of St Jeanne Antide, the Sisters of the Holy Cross, the Sisters of the Holy name of Jesus and the Sisters of the Resurrection. Also, as we have already seen, St David's home is run by the Sisters of Charity. All of these are within a half a mile radius of St Benedicts. It would be fair to say that there is quite a concentration of Catholic activity in the area and this could explain the popularity of Ealing for Catholic immigrants and there are large Polish, French and other Catholic communities in the Borough. Certainly St Benedicts, pictured below, is a very well supported church.

The purpose of these early chapters has been to set the scene and describe the surroundings of "Our House", the hinterland that will have been very familiar to the residents of 5 Queens Gardens and which, the golf club and the churches, they may well have used. As we shall shortly see the development of Queens Gardens began in 1901 and that is certainly the year in which our House was built. One is tempted to wonder what the first residents made of their new surroundings and whether they found it all quite confusing. To the south, barely half a mile away, was a monastery presumably with monks in their vestments. To the east, a couple of hundred yards away, a socialist, atheist (for a time anyway) enclave was taking shape. To the west, again just a couple of hundred yards away, was that ultimate symbol of the middle classes, a golf club. And to the north, half a mile away, was a graveyard that only the rich and famous could use. All of these were visible then from Queens Gardens, across fields and pastureland. And meanwhile all around were Royal references.

Now it is time to move from exploring the area generally to looking in detail at Our House and who occupied it. But first we will find out who built it, and we make the acquaintance of Thomas Richards, gentleman.

Chapter 9: Thomas Richards

Then, as now, you had to have to have Council permission to build houses and a perusal of the Minutes of the Council Works committee between 1898 and 1903 filled a very interesting afternoon. The committee met at least twice a month, sometimes more frequently. It was probably one of the most active Council functions as the breakneck expansion of Ealing took place. Charles Jones, who we have already met, would have been central to the meeting. *The edited minutes are shown below in italics* and my comments are in normal type.

- *May 18 1898 the committee noted a letter from Mr Ed Millard as to a report that cottages were to be erected on land north and east of the Mews, Castlebar Park. The committee decided it was nothing to do with them.* Ed Millard was part of the Millard family that owned Pitshanger farm and were highly interested in all developments in the area. Developers were competing for opportunities and the committee seems here to have decided they cannot favour one developer over another.

- *May 18 1898 Outline plans for "New Road", Pitshanger Lane were approved subject to lamp posts and hardcore not ballast foundations. July 5th 1898 amended plans for New Road Pitshanger lane were approved.* For Greenfield sites (literally in this case) the developer was responsible for supplying the facilities – roads, drains, water and so on. Until roads and houses were built and named they were often called "New Road" much as start-up companies these days are often called Newco. "New Road" Pitshanger Lane will become, as we shall see, Queens Gardens.

- *September 19th 1899 an estate plan was submitted by the Trustees of Mr Millard, Pitshanger estate, Woodfield Road, this was approved subject to lamp posts being marked on the plan and amended specifications as to the material being used.*

- *October 3rd 1899 under Estate Plans Mr Alex Green submitted plans for the "sewers etc" on the <u>east</u> side of Queens Walk and the <u>south</u> side of Pitshanger lane.* This must have been Queens Gardens. *The roads on this estate are approved subject to modifications of lamp posts and man holes and the question of building lines being referred back for further consideration. Final approval was given on 17th October 1899.* At this stage the committee appears to be happy with the infrastructure and the next stage is to get approval for the houses to be built.

- *3rd April 1900 Mr Thomas Richards is given approval for 14 houses in* (what is now) Queens Gardens.

- *15th May 1900 Mr Thomas Richards is given approval for 14 houses in Queens Walk "approval to be subject to vents on the fireplace in the small bedroom"*

- *15th May 1900 Mr Thomas Richards submits plans for 10 houses in Lyncroft gardens* (note – the road already has a name so there must have been houses already there) These are semi-detached although that was not recorded in the minutes and are virtually identical in all other respects, as we shall see, to Queens Walk and Gardens.

- *On July 24th 1900 a letter from Mr Richards complaining about conditions in Blakesley Avenue and asking that this road be taken over.* This is not in fact Thomas Richards, From the Law lists, of which more later, this is Frank Izod Richards (qualified 1880) of Treherne Higgins & co 7 Bloomsbury Square and 19 Blakesley Avenue, and no relation.

- One matter that crops up in all the minutes of every meeting is complaints about dust collections. Then, as now, rubbish collection was a major issue for residents. But rubbish in those days was different to today. There were no plastics, packaging was much less and food was not wasted; what was produced in industrial quantities was ash from coal burning fires. There was no central heating and cooking was on a fuel burning range and so, in our house, there would have been 7 or 8 open fires in winter and at least 1, for cooking, in summer. Multiply this throughout the Borough and that is a lot of ash and cinders to process.

- Nov 13th 1900 Plans submitted by the Richards estate for new roads and sewers on the Pitshanger and Woodbury estates, North Ealing, were approved subject to 6 inch Portland cement concrete to be provided under kerbs and channels in lieu of 4 inches as shown on the plans. Manholes to be provided at heads of surface water sewers.

- The above confirms that the developer pays for the roads and sewers needed for new houses.

- Feb 5th 1901 T Richards – 12 houses in Pitshanger lane approved subject to footings being brought up to 14 inches to ground floor joists and revised plan of drainage being sent in.

- Nov 18th 1902 The Borough Surveyor reported on the bad condition of Pitshanger lane and a letter is to be sent to the various owners calling upon them to repair the road. This crops up all the time – traffic is increasing and so is housing density.

- The last minutes in the minute book I saw were for May 3rd 1904 and so, by then a) the rest of the Queens Gardens development beyond the 14 houses approved had not started and b) Thomas Richards had made no further applications.

- And so, by May 1904 Thomas Richards had received approval to build at least 50 houses, 14 in Queens Gardens, 14 in Queens Walk, 10 in Lyncroft Gardens and 12 in Pitshanger lane, and, since "Our House" was built in 1901, he had made a start on them. It is time to see what we can find out about Thomas Richards.

After the problems with Henry de Bruno Austin 30 years earlier, Ealing, and Charles Jones as Surveyor, would surely not have given approval for 50 houses except to someone who clearly had the resources to see them completed successfully and that person would probably have had to have some influence as well. Thomas Richards had both of those qualities, as well as an interesting story.

Thomas Richards was a lawyer with his own practice as the following extract from the London Gazette of December 12 1902 attests. This is certainly the right Thomas Richards because the address below is the same as that in our title deeds. It was his firm because it is called "T Richards & Co." Edward John Southern, Richards' co-plaintiff in this case, is presumably a partner in his firm and he will crop up again in this story. In this particular case, which is nothing to do with our story, there appears to be a dispute between the executors of the deceased and the deceased's family.

Re JOHN REED HUBBARD, Deceased.
PURSUANT to an Order of the Chancery Division
of the High Court of Justice, dated the 30th
day of October, 1902, and made in the matter of the
estate of John Reed Hubbard, deceased, and in an action
SOUTHERN AND ANOTHER v. HUBBARD AND
OTHERS (1902; H. No. 1698), the creditors of John
Reed Hubbard, late of the Victoria Inn, Victoria-road,
Kingston-on-Thames, Surrey, Licensed Victualler (but
formerly a Fine Art Dealer and Print Seller), who died
on the 28th day of October. 1900, are, on or before the
17th day of January, Ifc03, to send by post, prepaid, to
Mr. Thomas Richards, of the firm of T. Richards and Co.,
of 31, York-place, Portman-square, in the county of
London, Solicitors for the plaintiffs, Edward John
Southern and Thomas Richards, the executors of the
deceased, their Christian and surname?, addresses and
descriptions, the full particulars of their claims, a statement
of their accounts, and the nature of the securities
(if any) held by them, or in default thereof they will be
peremptorily excluded from the benefit of the said Order.
Every creditor holding any security is to produce the
same before the Judge, in chambers, Room 689, the
Royal Courts of Justice, London, on the 2lst day of
January, 1903, at 12 o'clock noon, being the time
appointed for adjudicating the claims.—Dated this llth
day of December, 1902.
. • • ' T. RICHARDS and CO., 31, York-place, Portman-
•square, London, W.C., Solicitors for the Plain-
. tiffs.

The above was easily found on Google. But, initially, finding out more was difficult because Thomas Richards is such a common name. A search through the censuses using Ancestry gives thousands of them. There had to be another piece of information so as to be able to focus the search and Jonathan Oates, Ealing Library's archivist suggested the Law lists, Thomas Richards, of course, being a solicitor. The Law list is an annual directory of everyone involved in the Law; solicitors, barristers, judges and so on and the National Archives at Kew hold the annuals back into the 19th century.

At this point a small diversion will have later relevance. The writer spent a considerable amount of time trying to find 31 York Place, Portman Square. It is not marked on the A-Z and I had assumed it was a cul de sac or mews, too small to mark. I eventually discovered that York Place was incorporated into Baker Street in 1921, it was that part of Baker Street between the Marylebone Road and where Paddington Street joins it 300 yards to the south. When this was done the numberings were changed for the whole length of Baker Street and 31 York Place,

Portman Square became 109 Baker Street. The old sign below, still used on one of the mansion blocks, is the only clue to the previous identity of the road.

I discovered the above quite by chance in happening upon a web site where there was a lot of correspondence, given the renaming and renumbering, of the exact location of 221b Baker St, the home of Sherlock Holmes. Conan Doyle's story was, of course, written long before 1921.

Like so much of London the classic Regency properties are now overtaken by shops and offices but 109 Baker Street is about the only property in the road to which this hasn't happened, it is still offices. The Rolls Royce parked outside was entirely accidental although somehow in keeping. This was, and is, a wealthy area and famous residents included Joseph Hume MP, Nicolas Wiseman, Archbishop of Westminster and, from a blue plaque, William Pitt the younger. 109 Baker Street is pictured right.

As well as having his own law firm and an expensive property in the West End Thomas Richards was also the managing director of the Sceptre Investment Company. One of my avenues of research for this book was to circulate a letter to all the owner/occupants of the houses for which Richards was granted approval asking if they would share their title deeds with me to see what could be found. There was an excellent response. From several deeds we find that the Sceptre Investment Company is either the freeholder, which would mean the Millards had sold their interests by then, or, perhaps, the managing agents on behalf of the Millards and the paperwork has Thomas Richards signing as Managing Director. The address given is 44 Finsbury Square, presumably the offices of Sceptre and today, below, the offices of Bloombergs (this is the site, the current building dates from the 1950s) It is quite likely that Thomas Richards got the development idea from his role at Sceptre.

All sorts of questions about conflicts of interest arise and we shall explore these later. For now, it would seem that Thomas Richards will have satisfied the Works committee that he has the resources and influence to be awarded the right to build 50 houses in north Ealing, including ours. What then do we know of Thomas Richards?

Using the Law lists it was possible to refine census searches considerably. Thomas Richards was born circa 1863 in Paddington, London. In early censuses only age was asked for and not date of birth and since censuses were not always on the same date every 10 years the year of birth can sometimes be a bit "circa" but, as we shall see, this is definitely him. His parents were Frederick T Richards born in Exeter and Elizabeth Richards, born in Bristol. From the census information Frederick was a Butler and Elizabeth was a Lace cleaner. In the 1871 census Elizabeth, 47, Lace cleaner, is at 67 Star Street with Thomas, 9, and Elizabeth, 13. She is married but no husband is recorded which is consistent with his being an on-duty Butler, recorded wherever he was working. In 1881 they are at the same address and she is noted as a Butler's wife and Thomas, 19, is recorded as a trainee solicitor and general clerk, born in Paddington. 67 Star Street is pictured below.

This is curious. Butlers, especially family butlers, normally lived-in where they worked and did not marry or have children that would be a burden on their employers. One can only assume that Frederick was a butler at an embassy or perhaps the entertainment section of a government department. He must have been well paid to afford the rent of a perfectly respectable property like that on the following page. Also registered at this address were 2 cooks, a housekeeper, a laundress and a general servant. These surely were not his servants? Either these were servants where Frederick worked, and perhaps the Embassy (or whatever it was) owned the property or he was renting personally and subletting to meet the costs.

In the 1891 census the family are at 27 Paddington Green. Daughter Elizabeth has left home but father Frederick, 60, is now at home and has retired since he is recorded as "living in means" with wife, Elizabeth, age 68, and Thomas Richards, 29, solicitors articled clerk. As we shall see within a year of this Thomas will have qualified. This is quite late to qualify. These days if you go straight from school you can expect to qualify in your mid-20s but now he really accelerates .and within 10 years he will have set up his own firm and then soon after that he is into property development. It was a real "Upstairs Downstairs" story. Number 27 Paddington Green has disappeared and lies beneath the City of Westminster College on Paddington Green which, itself, is the tiny scrap of green noticed on your left as you prepare to go over the Marylebone flyover heading into London. It was probably a charming area 100 years ago.

In the 1901 census he is 38 and a Solicitor (and "employer") living at 45 Queens Road Hampstead, with his wife Madge Richards ("Madge" implies a no-nonsense sort of household), age 27 (born 1874) from Nottingham, together with 2 servants, Susan Storey parlour maid, 25, and Alice Wood, cook, 24. As we shall see below he started his own firm in this very census year and so was an employer. It has not been possible to pin

down 45 Queens Road Hampstead for certain, perhaps it has been renamed or, more likely, redeveloped but the picture below was found on the English Heritage web site "Images for learning" the National Monument Record. It says 45 Queens Road, St John's Wood, not Hampstead. However Hampstead is the older London suburb and was probably the name of the area in 1901. But by 1916 when the picture was taken St John's Wood was developing and had presumably given its name to this smaller area. There are no other addresses that could fit the criteria. The same thing happened to Richards' office. In the census it was 31 York Place, Portman Square. But it is at least half a mile from Portman Square. This demonstrates the rapid expansion of London at the time. As new areas were developed they acquired new names. Today 109 Baker Street would be thought of as Marylebone, the High Street is just 100 yards away, not Portman Square. Assuming this is 45 Queens Road Thomas Richards had obviously moved elsewhere by 1916. The property is clearly a significant one. I did at one time consider entitling the book "From Queens Road to Queens Gardens"

"A portrait of Mrs Freeman, reclining on a couch in the sitting room of 45 Queen's Road, St John's Wood. This photograph was commissioned by Mrs Freeman herself"

Having been through the Law lists from 1890 to 1930 whilst there are several other Richards' there is no other Thomas Richards and so this must be him. In 10 years he has gone from living with his parents in servant's quarters to Hampstead employing his own servants. Thomas did not come from a privileged background or, probably, a prestigious school but just had to work up the hard way. Going through the Law lists in more detail we find the following.

In the **1892** list there is no mention of him but as we shall see later he qualifies in May 1892. There is mention of a Thomas James Savage (Qualified June 1886) at 57 +59 Ludgate hill and Chiswick. In **1893** Thomas Richards is shown at G R Browne & Co 13 Church Ct Ironmonger Lane and 28 Fordwych Road Brondersbury (now Kilburn) where he may have lived for a while. In **1895** he is at Savage Richards & Co 44 Finsbury Sq and 28 Fordwych Road. In **1896** he is at Finsbury Square and in **1897** also at Red Tower Chambers, High Road, Kilburn. From **1898 – 1900** he is just at Finsbury Square and then in **1901,** with the birth of a new century, his new company is launched, Thomas Richards & Co, 31 York Place, Portman square and it is in this year, because he is now a principle, that the date of his qualification is show. By **1903** his company still exists but it appears he is no longer practising, his name does not appear in the firm and it stays this way for the next 17 years. He still owns the firm but appears preoccupied by other things and we shall discover that property development was one of those.

In **1920** T.Richards & Co is re-energised by the return of Thomas Richards as well as the appointment of 3 new partners George Henry Lowthian, William James Williams and Charles Henry Read and the address is 31 York Place, **Baker Street,** not Portman Square, in anticipation of the change to come. Then in **1921** the address is shown as 109 Baker Street and in **1926** T Richards & co take on a further 4 partners and it remains this way until 1939. By **1994** T Richards & Co is still going but is now at 96 Gloucester Place W1H 3DA and there are no Richards' as partners.

The picture below is not Thomas Richards but is how a solicitor would have looked in those days.

Thomas Richards died on November 14th 1952 aged 91. In a local paper there is an announcement that "he died very peacefully in a nursing home at 10 Eaton Gardens, Hove, Sussex. He was a retired solicitor and founder of T Richards & Co of 109 Baker street" The announcement also says that "cars will be at Hove station to meet the 10am train from Victoria" Clearly a large number of his former Law and City friends were expected (and, as we shall see below, it is highly likely that all staff at T. Richards & Co were given the day off to say goodbye to their founder)

When I started this research it felt like a historical exercise into a long gone Victorian gentleman from another era. It was quite a surprise to find that we overlapped, albeit only for 5 or 6 years, which brings history and the present day into perspective.

The terms of his will, dated 14th October 1950, are interesting. It starts "I, Thomas Richards of 42 Sackville Gardens, Hove, in the County of Sussex, retired Solicitor and formerly well known when in practice as a Solicitor at 109 Baker Street, London W1" It then states that this will supersedes all previous ones (this could mean that his wife died in 1950 necessitating a new will, it is difficult to imagine a Solicitor preparing his first will at the age of 87) and it appointed as executors Edward Athol Taylor, Peter Athol Taylor and James Frederick Stephenson, all partners in T. Richards & Co. Other than a number of specific bequests it then left the entire estate to these three. The specific bequests were; to his niece Elsie Burr, £4500, his freehold house at 58 Mazenod Avenue, Kilburn to his chauffeur, John Horrell, the leasehold premises at 109 Baker Street to Edward Athol Taylor and to his nurse Edith Neal, £200, "to be increased to £500 if she shall be in my service at the date of my death" After these everything else is left to the executors including his previous Hove residence of 42 Sackville Gardens. There is no mention of family other than the niece so presumably his wife had predeceased him and they had no children. The will was realised on the 3rd February 1953 which is very quick given that they had property to dispose of. Of the gross value of the estate of £63174 6s 3d estate duty removed £23680. Using property prices as a gauge his estate would have been worth about £6 million in today's values although on other measures it could have been 3 or even 4 times as much as this; giving a house to your chauffeur is indicative of the size of his estate.

It is difficult to know how to regard his will. It seems extraordinarily profligate of him not to have done some estate planning to reduce the tax burden, almost unprofessional. It is as though he did not know what to do with all his wealth and ended up giving most of it to the Inland Revenue and to the 3 partners in his firm who were almost certainly very rich people anyway and did not need it. Was he perhaps so work obsessed that he had no life outside of that and therefore nowhere else to leave his fortune? Or is it possible that when his wife, Madge, died, he lost his driving force and simply did not know what he wanted to do? Couldn't he perhaps have left something to charity or even the nursing home that looked after him? He left considerably more to his (work related) chauffeur than to his (blood related) niece. But, as the son of a Butler and Lace cleaner from a small Paddington house Thomas Richards had nonetheless done extraordinarily well.

There are many intriguing aspects to Thomas' story but perhaps above all, his wife. "Madge" (presumably Margaret) from Nottingham, 8 years younger than him, seems an unlikely union for an about-to-be qualified London solicitor. Was she a forced marriage from amongst the domestics at Star Street? If so I have not located a child. Alternatively perhaps she was the ambitious one and spurred him on perhaps taking on more than he should have? In 1881 Thomas was 19 and a trainee solicitor and general clerk. It then took him 11 years to finally qualify in 1892, was she the catalyst? In fact perhaps she pushed him too far? The near 20 year break (between 1903 and 1920) which he took from his own firm, just a few years after he had started it, may well have been because he overextended himself both financially (with his property investments as well as taking on 31 York Place and he needed time to sort all of this out) as well as in time (with his commitments to Sceptre as well) There does seem to be reason to believe that not all of his property speculations in Ealing were successful and we will now turn to those property developments.

In his original dealings with Ealing's works committee Richards was given permission to build 50 houses – 14 in Queens Gardens, 14 in Queens Walk, 10 in Lyncroft Gardens and 12 in Pitshanger lane. In the event he only built 9 of the 14 approved in Queens Gardens, 6 of the 14 in Queens Walk, he did build all 10 approved in Lyncroft Gardens but he built none of those approved in Pitshanger Lane; in total 25 out of the 50 approved, perhaps his property development business proved more troublesome than expected. He may have run out of money (although he presumably had Sceptre behind him) or it may be that it did not turn out to be the financial bonanza he had hoped for. I do not know the order in which the developments took place but it is interesting that Lyncroft Gardens was completed and not the others. The reason for this could be that being in south Ealing, much more populous than north Ealing then, these properties were much more saleable. And it is also possible that some or perhaps all, for this reason, were presold; there is internal evidence in some of the houses of tailoring for the wishes of the buyers (I was told by one resident that "similar houses along our side of Lyncroft Gardens each can have slightly different configurations; we have been told that original purchasers were able to choose whether to have 4 or 5 bedrooms. Our front hall floor is wooden; another in the road has original decorative clay tiles on a solid floor. No doubt each house may have small differences) If they were presold then it would be difficult to stop the building if deposits had been paid. But from their location they were likely to have been profitable anyway. The other 3 developments in north Ealing would be a different matter.

But first, having got his council approvals, Thomas will have had to raise the finance. Whilst he was clearly a prosperous man he appears to have wanted to do almost everything personally so as to benefit to the greatest extent and this will have been like having 50 (eventually 25) mortgages. To an extent this will have been manageable by building 1 or 2 and then selling them and using the proceeds to finance the next 1 or 2 and so on. But the Council's approval was unlikely to have been completely open ended and there will have been some time limit. He would need partners to share the debt burden but without giving too much away and, as we shall see, this is what he did. The fact that he only built 25 out the planned 50 may have been because he ran out of time within the Council's approvals, or because the debt proved too onerous or because the houses, especially the north Ealing ones, proved less profitable than expected or a combination of all of these.

We will now bid farewell to Thomas Richards personally and turn, in the next chapter, to the 25 properties he built and then, in the chapter after that we will do a finance report on his property business before then turning to the occupants of one of those properties, namely, Our House.

Chapter 10: The Houses

Thomas Richards almost certainly had no experience in property development; he will have seen it purely as a potentially profitable speculation. The three developments he did complete are all essentially in the same style but it is unlikely this was a style he created. More likely the style was simply chosen from a London pattern book which existed at that time, and, quite possibly also, he was guided by Charles Jones, the Borough Surveyor, who may have wanted a little balancing up after approving the workers cottages of the Brentham estate. And in fact the Richards houses could not be a greater contrast to the Brentham houses. The market for the Richards houses was prosperous middle class professionals not artisans.

The houses were built in a villa style, more mini-Downton Abbey than maxi-Brentham estate and they have 10 feet high ceilings, tradesman's entrances and provision for live-in domestic staff. They must have been expensive to build and this may explain the problems in selling them.

If the style we will look at below is a standard pattern then it is not one that is used very often. Other than the 25 we will look at below I have seen no others in Ealing. There are some similar but not identical ones in Chevening Road, Kilburn and in Harrow but it is certainly not a design that is commonly seen.

There is an interesting fragment on one set of drawings shown below.

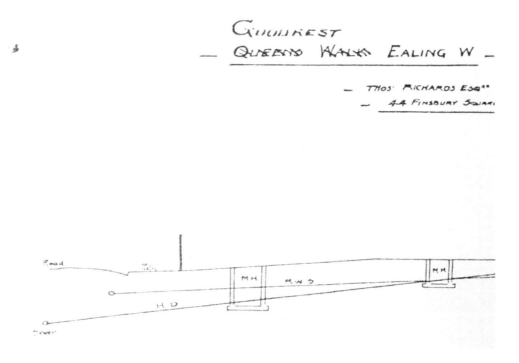

These were drawings for the Queens Walk properties and in this plan Queens Walk is crossed out and replaced by Goodrest which is how Lyncroft Gardens was known whilst under development. One set of plans may have sufficed for all three sites. The detailed plans are very interesting and now follow. The houses in Lyncroft Gardens are semidetached and those in Queens Walk and Gardens are detached but in all other respects they are identical. The plans below were courtesy of David in Lyncroft Gardens. There are probably no houses now that look exactly like the plans below; over the years we have all extended and taken walls down and the design of the houses has been very accommodating to do just this. The ground floor plans are shown below and don't forget this shows 2 houses.

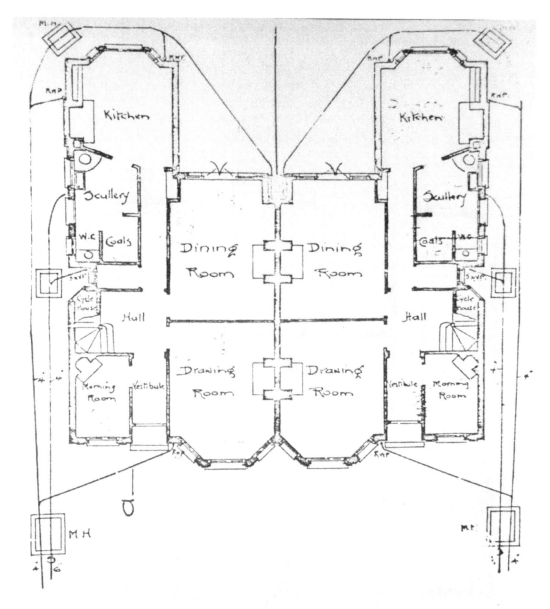

There are several things to note here. After entering the front door there is a small morning room, with an open fire, immediately off the vestibule. In our house (and others I have seen) there is no sign of there having been such a wall, the morning room and hall are all one space; evidence of tailoring the houses for individual tastes? Continuing on into the hall notice the cycle house under the stairs and accessed from the side passage. When the houses were built there were no motorised vehicles for another 10 years and transport was either pony and trap, and some certainly had these, bicycles, shanks' pony or the newly arrived underground train system but you had to get to Ealing Broadway first. As we move on into the kitchen we come into an area designed for servants. The kitchen and scullery were the workplace of the maid and the WC was for her use. Note that coal stocks were kept indoors (we keep ours in the cycle house). With so many fireplaces in the house and a relatively small storage area they must have needed almost weekly coal deliveries in the winter. The external door in the scullery is the tradesman's entrance and our door still has the original door knocker, pictured below. Most of these side passages have now been covered over to create extra space.

In our house, and probably most others, the scullery walls have all been removed and the kitchen opened up. We have also taken down the wall between the dining room and drawing room.

Because I had never thought about it the discovery of provision for servants, especially live-in domestic staff, came as quite a surprise. In 1900 1.3 million workers were in domestic service, perhaps nearly 10% of the working population. This percentage will have been higher in the prosperous cities. It was not just nobility that had staff; it extended right down to the lower middle classes. After the First World War this percentage declined quickly, especially after modern appliances started to appear; central heating, washing machines and so on. Now we move to the first floor pictured below in the original plans.

The servant's bedroom could have been any of them but was probably the small back bedroom; there is evidence in at least one house in Lyncroft Gardens of a reduced quality of wall finish and doors for the back bedroom.

Note that all the bedrooms have fireplaces. In winter there would have been 8 or 9 fireplaces to attend to every day.

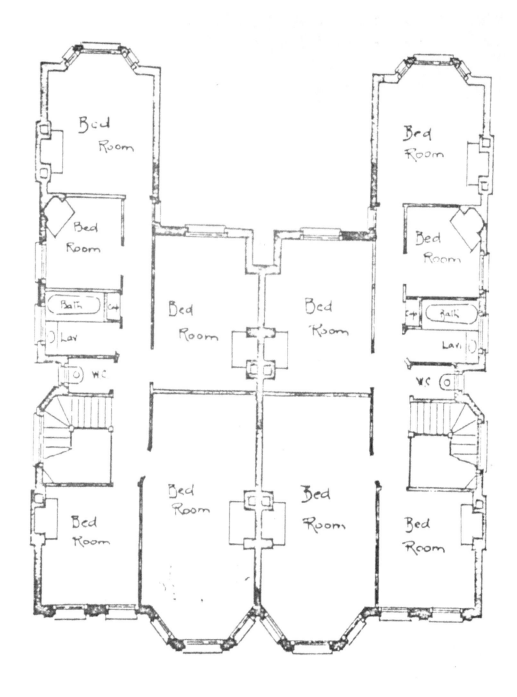

Now we will look at each of the 3 developments.

Lyncroft Gardens

This development opportunity arose because James Berry decided to sell some of the land surrounding his large house "Goodrest" He will have been aware of the encroaching suburban development all around him and eventually decided to capitalise on it. But to preserve his property (now demolished) he sold the land with provisos restricting building any closer than 50 yards of the cross roads where his house was and with conditions that only private dwelling houses can be built and that the houses built should be of a value of at least £400. If he had to have neighbours he did not want riff raff.

The land for Lyncroft Gardens was conveyed on 27th May 1896 between (1) James Berry (mortgagee of the land), and (2) Charles Johnstone Burt and Thomas Richards the joint purchasers of the land. On the land conveyance Thomas Richards gave his address as 44 Finsbury Square, which were of course the offices of Sceptre Investment Co, but he and Burt bought in their personal capacities. Charles Johnstone Burt was the secretary of the Westbourne Park Permanent Building society and, as such, a very useful business partner to have. The 10 houses were built between 1901 and 1907.

In the case of two of the properties (and perhaps more than two, perhaps all) the financing of the deal was interesting. What Richards and Burt had originally bought was a head lease. The land to be developed had presumably been farmland until then and therefore probably itself leasehold with the freehold owned by The Sceptre Investment Company. In a lease dated 24th June 1901 (when these two houses had, presumably, been completed) Richards and Burt grant Edward John Southern (a Director of Sceptre Investment Co) a lease for the properties. To finance this one day later on the 25th June Southern takes a mortgage with the Westbourne Park Permanent Building Society (of which Burt is the secretary) for both properties. Then on 30th September 1904 Southern sells one of the leases back to Richards. In all of these transactions the solicitors are, of course, T Richards & Co. Thomas Richards has successfully used his connections and their ability to sustain debt to develop more than he might have been able to do on his own. They have done all this in their personal capacities despite the conflicts of interest that would arise today with their employers; Thomas Richards with his own firm and Sceptre Investment Co, Charles Johnstone Burt with the Westbourne Park Permanent Building Society and Edward John Southern with Sceptre Investment Co.

There is evidence in Lyncroft Gardens of individual houses having slightly different configurations; indeed it is believed that original purchasers were able to choose whether to have 4 or 5 bedrooms. One house has a front hall floor that is wooden; another in the road has original decorative clay tiles on a solid floor. This makes it likely that the houses were presold and could incorporate individual preferences.

One of the houses, it is believed, was built by the builder of the Lyncroft houses for his own daughter's use. It had a double length garden, and contains an unmade lane which runs back behind the rear gardens to exit in Waldemar Road. The lane was originally carriage access for the rear of the house and there is evidence of where stables would have been for the horse. There is no evidence of service roads and stables for horses and carriages in either Queens Walk or Gardens but subsequent development may have submerged these.

There are a number of interesting features in Lyncroft Gardens including an original servant's bell push (right)

There is also a theory that the way the doors opened in the above plans confirmed that the house were designed for servants since the doors always opened away from the room so as to warn residents of the imminent entry of a servant.

As well as the title deeds the residents of Lyncroft also gave a number of interesting anecdotes. From Derek and Alison "We believe the upstairs rear bedroom may have been a servant's room, and the box-room for the servant's personal use. The upstairs hall corridor has a ceiling feature which may well be where a door led to the servant's 2 rooms" and "similar houses along our side of Lyncroft Gardens each can have slightly different configurations; we have been told (by Judith we think) that original purchasers were able to choose whether to have 4 or 5 bedrooms. Our front hall floor is wooden; another in the road has original decorative clay tiles on a solid floor. No doubt each house may have small differences"

Queens Walk

Lyncroft Gardens is in south Ealing and now we move to the much more recently developed north Ealing and houses which may well have been far harder to sell. My letter to residents did not elicit any title deeds information but did produce some delightful anecdotes.

Lucy and Bernard wrote "*Our house was built in 1910 or 1911. When we came the land opposite (where University Court now stands) was an orchard and to the left an accommodation block for nurses from West Middlesex Hospital I think. The orchard was in use regularly by a fellow called Graham, a fruit and vegetable merchant who came round with his lorry to do house-to-house sales. He kept the grass down by buying clapped out horses or ponies from the weekly horse fair in Southall, fattening them up to sell on. There were also chickens if I remember rightly. Graham kept his lorry in Castlebar Mews which really was a mews with garages which had all the hallmarks of stables even then* (stables to perhaps serve residents of Queens Walk and Queens Gardens?) *The present flats were built some 10 years later*"

The picture below, dated 1929 confirms that the land opposite was arable at least until then. The widespread use of horses and carriages in the area is confirmed by the horse trough which still exists at Haven Green and is pictured on the next page. This one was donated by Walter Wilson in 1898, just as north Ealing was being developed and residents would need access to the station.

Queens Walk in 1929

Horse trough at Haven Green.

64

Another neighbour commented: *"The first house in Queens Walk was then occupied by the Golinski family and was much like the other houses except that the walls facing Queen's Gardens were extended and had little side windows, as now. Golinski built on the additional rooms on the garden side, built an outside staircase (on the other side of the house in the picture below) for the flats above and removed the staircase inside. (He was keen to maximise his assets, so made 4 flats.) The loft extension was added when a Mr Luther or Mr Lutter owned the property (before current planning regulations were in place) I went over the house during its refurbishment, which was awful. The builder confided in me that he was ashamed to be asked to do such a jerry-build job"*

The house is pictured below. One shudders to think what Thomas Richards or even Charles Jones would have made of such an unsympathetic conversion, one of very few conversions to Richards houses in these three areas.

Peter in Queens Walk wrote a sadder story. *"Our house in Queens Walk was put on the market in 2003, when at the time we lived further down the road and it was being lived in by an elderly, and clearly physically and mentally unwell, gentleman. We viewed the house at that time and it was in a semi-derelict state. The garden was a jungle, and the inside of the house was in a dilapidated state. It was too big a job for us to take on. Developers bought the property. In January of 2004 whilst the developers were in early stages of renovation we agreed to purchase the house from them and they finished renovating the house under our direction. Whilst I was visiting the site on an occasion in January, the chap leading the building team excitedly showed me an old photo album which he had discovered under piles of rubbish in the attic. The old gentleman who was living in the house prior to its sale had lived here with his Sister all of his life and was now into his late 80s. The album contains many pictures of him as a young child, playing in the garden in the 1920s. There is a beautiful rose arch in the pictures, which, in 2004 before the garden was cleared, you could still detect under the mass of 12 foot bindweed. There it was still, twisted and broken, and probably with the same rose bush from 80 years ago which was struggling under the weight of the vegetation and weeds that had overwhelmed it. The rose arch physically linked the fresh new garden of then in the photograph with the overgrown dereliction of now, reflecting too the man inside the house, who when we viewed the house was hunched over a 2 bar electric fire. His nephew sold the property though I doubt the elderly gentleman was in agreement. Apparently he died soon after leaving this house, his family home of 80 years"*

Queens Gardens

This is our road and we will be coming to Our House soon. I have been able to trace more of the early transactions than in the other two.

On 29th November 1900 a 99 year lease was signed between The Sceptre Investment Company (of 3 Church court, Old Jewry, signed by E J Southern, Director) and Thomas Richards at an annual rent of £10. On 1st December 1900 Thomas Richards , "gentleman", of 31 York Place, Portman Square, entered a mortgage with the Boatmans Institution & General Mutual Benefit Building Society, Sale Street, Paddington (TR's old stamping ground) for £1200 for the building of numbers **3 and 5** Queens Gardens. There is a map attached showing the plot sizes for numbers 1-11. Number 5 is 30ft 0inches wide and 140ft 10 inches long, this is 469.444 sq. feet or about a tenth of an acre. Both documents were prepared by T Richards & Co.

What Thomas Richards bought was a head lease. The land to be developed had presumably been farmland until then and therefore probably itself leasehold with the freehold owned by The Sceptre Investment Company of which he was managing director.

In the Kelly's directory for 1900/1 there is no mention of Queens Gardens but they were usually about a year out of date when published. The 1901 census also shows nothing for Queens Gardens so construction presumably started soon after. Kelly's for 1902 showed numbers 1, 5 and 7 Queens Gardens but not number 3 or 9 onwards which were presumably still under construction, with an Albert Boehr (the subject of the next chapter but one) occupying number

5. He was still there in 1903/4 and by then there were numbers 1 – 15 Queens Gardens, and he was still there in 1905/6.

On 7th June 1906 5 Queens Gardens were assigned by Thomas Richards and the Boatmans Institute to Frank William Handover. He paid £500 for the remainder of the lease. His mortgage was repayable partly on a repayment system and partly on a standing mortgage system by monthly payment and it gave the right to sublet. We saw above that Richards had taken a £1200 mortgage to build numbers 3 and 5, presumably representing £600 building costs for each, and now he is selling one of them 4 years later for £500, this sounds like bad business. Frank William Handover, as we shall see, only owned the property for a short period and never lived in it himself so presumably was also a speculator and saw his chance. And there is another example. In neighbour Patrick's title deeds we find Edward John Southern, a Director of Sceptre Investment Co, taking a 99 year lease from the Sceptre Investment Company and a £500 mortgage from the Westbourne Park Permanent building society in June 1903, which is then assigned by Southern to Richards in September 1906 and then Richards mortgages the same property in October 1916 for £350. The mortgage is presumably to raise funds for other developments but it sounds as if the value of the properties has gone down dramatically. The reasons for Thomas Richards not completing his Queens Gardens and Queens Walk developments become clear, he is building houses that are too large and too expensive and, for the time being, in the wrong place.

If my interpretation above is correct then Richards may have lost a considerable amount of money. From his sale to Handover he lost £100 on a £600 investment or 17%. Multiply this by all 15 houses in Queens Gardens and Walk and express this in today's monetary values and you get well over a million pounds. If the remortgage in 1916 for £350 is a closer representation of values then it is several millions. Lyncroft Gardens are likely to have been less of a financial disaster and he may have made a small profit to offset the other losses. Lyncroft, being semis, will have been somewhat cheaper to build, much easier to sell being in a more established part of Ealing and Richards will probably not have had to pay for the road and drainage to be installed for the same reason.

As well as losing money Richards may also have lost friends. For several of the houses Edward John Southern, Richards' partner, gets the mortgage and buys the development to then later sell it back to Richards. I had originally interpreted this as Richards spreading the financing burden amongst friends and then taking the properties back when he could refinance and leaving them with something for their efforts. In fact it may be that Southern (and there may be others I haven't discovered) simply wanted out of a bad investment and triggered some sort of put arrangement.

We saw in the previous chapter that Richards, having set up his new firm, then did not practice from 1903 to 1920, at which time he took on 3 new partners. This is consistent with his mind having been elsewhere sorting out a disaster. There are similarities with Henry de Bruno Austin and his ambitious schemes but, at least, Richards avoided bankruptcy and ended his life a very rich man. Much later, as we came to buy our property, the solicitors were briefly concerned about a restrictive covenant against 5 Queens Gardens namely "A conveyance dated 16th November 1865 between Charles Paul Millard and Henry De Bruno Austin containing restrictive covenants but neither the original conveyance nor a certified copy was produced on first registration" We have come across Henry de Bruno Austin before and he crops up in each of the other areas as well and for all the Richards properties in Queens Gardens. These are probably call options giving Austin the first call when the land is to be sold. The options will have fallen away with his bankruptcy. We will examine Thomas Richards' financial position in the next chapter.

Even if the houses were a financial failure for Thomas Richards he has left a legacy of beautiful houses and many of us still have original features such as the door furniture (right) in our houses.

Pitshanger Lane

Thomas Richards did not start any of the houses for which he had permission in Pitshanger Lane. Instead this road developed a different function. With so much development in north Ealing there would eventually have to be a shopping area, people couldn't keep going down to central Ealing for their shopping and this will, of course, have been a commercial opportunity and so Pitshanger Lane developed into the heart of this part of north Ealing.

There was only 1 shop in Pitshanger Lane in 1906 – the Co-operative stores at numbers 40 and 41. Unless the numbering has changed it is now Pizza Piccolo and is at the furthest western extremity of the shopping parade on the north side. The stores are pictured below circa 1918 and it is interesting that the Coop then were outfitters as well as grocers.

Picture reproduced by permission of Ealing Library

For the Coop to be the first to come seems appropriate in view of the cooperative, socialist experiment that had started on the Brentham estate; did Henry Vivian persuade them to come? But the stores were a long way from the Brentham estate, in fact at the wrong end of the Lane. The reason for this may well have been that Pitshanger farm, at the other end of the parade, supplied retail foodstuffs, and there was no sense in being too close to them. In any event the Coop has prospered and now has 2 large stores at either end of the Lane thus, perhaps, preserving the link with those Fabian days.

Pitshanger today and in 1909, with some shops just visible, are pictured below. As the shops multiplied many were owned and run by tenants from the Brentham estate thereby accelerating the trend we saw in chapter 6 of the estate quickly changing from a workers cooperative into a middle class suburb. Certainly by the start of the First World War Pitshanger Lane had a full complement of shops and resources to satisfy the newly developing area of north Ealing. In fact it has been a very successful shopping area and has developed an almost village feel which it tenaciously defends against the multiple stores.

Pitshanger Lane today.

Pitshanger Lane in 1909.

And so now we leave Thomas Richards and the styling of the houses he built and it is time to examine whether he made any money from his enterprises before we concentrate on one of the houses and its occupants – 'OUR' HOUSE.

Chapter 11: The Economics

The economics of Thomas Richards' business dealings are very interesting and more than a little bit scary. All his transactions were done in the currency of 1900 and so we will need to convert these to get an idea of what he was doing. Conveniently, a ready reckoner to convert 1900 prices to those of the present day is a factor of 1000. The average good costing £1 in 1900 costs £1000 today. The problem with this, however, is that it is an average. Within the average some things have gone up in price, relatively, and some have gone down. Property is undoubtedly one that has outperformed the average. Thomas Richards sold our house in 1906 for £600. That is £600,000 in today's money, about half its actual current value. Home ownership was much less common back then and the rise in its popularity has coincided with a growing population, shortage of land, and rising building costs, especially labour. The index for property could easily be double the figure above.

For all of the properties he developed Richards bought a 99 year lease; Sceptre were the freeholders. The cost of this lease was an innocuous sounding £10 per annum. But in today's terms this is equivalent to £10,000 per annum. Multiply this by 25 houses and that is £250,000 per annum. When the property was built and the 99 year lease sold to the purchaser this ground rent went with it. The key for Richards therefore, having got the Council's planning permission, would be to only buy the long lease from Sceptre when he was ready to build, and preferably had a buyer, and then to build as quickly as he possibly could, and within budget and then sell the property quickly.

There was no provision for escalation of the ground rent; it was fixed at £10 per annum for 99 years. This was a period when inflation was almost unknown, prices did sometimes go up but they also went down. Sceptre's return on their ground rent would have been, in today's terms, £1 million on every property (£10 x 99 years x 1000) In the event the 20th century invented inflation and leaseholders were buying out their freeholds in the 1950s and 1960s at very nominal amounts. But for Richards, the developer, he could not rely on the traditional modern view that house prices are bound to go up so just wait to get your money back; he would make his money if he processed each house quickly, built efficiently and if he had chosen an area that would be popular and easy to sell.

This chapter is his Finance Director's report on what he achieved.

In November//December 1900 TR bought the lease from Sceptre and took a mortgage for £1200 to build 3 and 5 Queens Gardens i.e. a £600 building cost for each. Our house probably took about a year to build. We will see in the next chapter that TR couldn't sell the lease until 1906 when he assigned it to Frank Handover for £600. On the face of it he has at least got his costs back and is only out of pocket for 5 years of ground rent (£50, or £50,000 which he probably won't have been able to recover from his tenants – see next chapter) But there are reasons to believe this transaction was not what it seems. Prices were falling. A neighbour's house (identical to ours) sold for £500 in 1903. In 1910 Handover assigned his lease to W Burnham for £490. Either Handover was gullible and TR talked him into paying too much, or they had some sort of side agreement whereby Handover relieved the strain on TR's finances. If so, he must have been a good and trusting friend. Handover is described in the documents as a surveyor and he would therefore surely not be gullible as to property. He lived throughout at 14a Pembridge

Road Notting Hill and he never lived in 5 Queens Gardens. He took a mortgage from the Westbourne Park BS to pay for his £600 assignment but only for £500, so he paid £100 (£100,000) out of his own pocket and was therefore presumably rich himself. I would strongly believe, with little evidence, that he was helping TR over some cash crunch by taking the property off his hands for an inflated amount, in effect giving him a loan. And this was the way to do it, a simple loan would have ranked below all the other debts TR had, doing it this way his assistance was secured to the property. But this only deferred TR's cash crunch which will have rematerialized in 1910 when Handover sold for £490, a cash loss of £110 (£110,000) without even counting the ground rent which may not have been covered by rents. If my interpretation is correct then TR will have had to make good Handover's losses. Naturally if you multiply this by 25 houses you get to some horrifying figures, but, as we've seen, Lyncroft Gardens probably washed it's face, or better, and it is only the 15 Queens Walk/Gardens properties where he may have had problems. But multiplying the above figures by 15 is scary enough. Neighbour Patricks house was built in the name of Edward Southern, a colleague of TR's in 1903 (the planning permission was in the name of TR so this presumably needed some sort of side agreement) and then sold back to TR in 1906 presumably realising losses similar to those above which, again, TR will have had to make good.

One imagines that TR had a vast spiders web matrix of agreements perhaps with many others not covered here and that constructing this will have taken much time but perhaps not as much as managing and deconstructing it. TR must have sailed close to bankruptcy and certainly lost a considerable amount of money on Queens Walk/Gardens and extracting himself from all this is surely why he took 17 years off from his newly established legal practice (but which he continued to own) as we saw in the previous chapter.

His fundamental problem was timing. He was building large houses in the middle of green fields that only the prosperous professional classes could afford (with ground rents of £10 pa, £10,000 today) but his plans were formed in 1899 or before and before he knew it the Brentham estate was being built and his houses were not in the middle of green fields but in the middle of a building site. Add to this how far the houses were from necessary facilities; shops, trains and so on and it would be 10 – 15 years before the purchasers he had imagined started to buy the houses, as the building was complete and as Pitshanger Lane became the local shopping centre and as local buses appeared. All rather late for TR! He did considerably worse building upwards than Charles Hughes did digging downwards at St Mary's church!

What then do we make of TR as a person? All of the facts about him known to me are contained herein so this is purely speculation. He came from a modest but not humble background. We have seen how it took him an unusually long time to qualify as a solicitor but then he moved very quickly to start his own company and move into property development as well as being Managing Director of Sceptre. Something energised him and it could well have been his wife, Madge. He then lost a lot of money but by the end of his life had made a lot of money. But then, at the end of his life, he didn't know what to do with his fortune and gave it to people who didn't need it and, tellingly, for the most part gave it colleagues at his company, almost as if once Madge had gone he had no direction and his life anyway had been the business to the exclusion of everything else.

We now take our leave of Thomas Richards and turn to the occupants of Our House.

Chapter 12: Albert Boehr 1901-06

The first houses to be built in the Queens Gardens/Walk complex were numbers 3 and 5 (our house) Queens Gardens in 1901. For the briefest of moments the occupiers must have thought they were in heaven. For a while they were surrounded by fields and with clear views of Horsenden hill and perhaps Harrow on the hill, the golf club and the Benedictine monastery and St Mary's. But not for long if at all.

It would not be long before the area resembled a building site. Firstly there were the other Richards properties going up all around them. But this was almost certainly compounded by the development of the Brentham estate. We saw earlier that 600 houses were built between 1901 and 1915, more than 40 houses a year. The building materials for all this construction, bricks, concrete, timber and so on, will all have been delivered by horse and cart with much of it having been landed at Brentford docks. The most direct way from the docks to the Brentham estate, at least for the first 5 years or so, will have been along Queens Gardens. Pitshanger Lane until much later was just a farm track that did not extend eastwards beyond the farmhouse. So Thomas Richards will have paid for Queens Gardens to be laid only to find it taken over by Henry Vivian for his development. But more importantly all that traffic and construction will have made the new properties very difficult to sell and they were going to be a hard sell anyway being so far away from everyday facilities and shops. In fact Thomas Richards could not sell our house and had to rent it out until the area quietened down and developed. It is highly likely that the rent he obtained was nominal and did not cover his costs, this conclusion follows from the first tenant who was not the typical occupier Thomas Richards might have hoped for.

The first tenant was Albert Boehr and his family. Albert Edward Boehr was born in Danzig, Prussia in about 1845/6. Today Danzig is in Poland not Prussia and Prussia is part of Germany. He is recorded as having arrived at Dover as an alien arrival on 30th June 1851, aged about 6. The country of origin is noted as Austria. There is no record of any parents and he is noted as having a passport from the Austrian Government. He was almost certainly caught up in the revolutions that broke out throughout Europe in 1848. There were uprisings in Italy, Poland, France, Germany and Austria. The main causes of the revolutions were widespread dissatisfaction with political leadership; demands for more participation in government and democracy; the demands of the working classes and, crucially, an upsurge of nationalism. Albert Boehr must have got caught up in all this and become separated from his family, or perhaps they were killed. The Austrian passport presumably was because he was retrieved by an Austrian equivalent of the Red Cross. Over its 1000 year history Danzig has been about half the time part of Prussia and the other half part of Poland. The revolutions did not reach Russia, Great Britain, Spain, Sweden or Portugal and displaced people made for or were sent to these countries as well as the USA. There are a lot of Boehrs in Wisconsin who were born circa the 1850s. Boehr is not a common German name but Boehringer is quite common and the names may have been shortened by the authorities.

So Albert Boehr came to England in 1851, aged about 6, and presumably was brought up in an orphanage or by foster parents. The next record we have of him is when he married. In 1870 Albert married Frances Sophia (maiden name unknown) who had been born in Cambridge in about 1840; she was 30 and he was 25. This may have been when he got his nationality. It may also have been a marriage of convenience; he was a German foster child, by then surely completely anglicised but needing a nationality, and she was unmarried at 30? If this is true then it appeared to work out because they had many children.

In 1881 he is 35 and they are living at 3 Belgrave Terrace in Lewisham and he is "Manager Civil Service S.A." S.A may be Staff Association and sounds a responsible job. Frances is 42 and they have 5 children at the time although, as we shall see, there are more to come.

- Otto (10) – August Albert O (presumably Otto, now dropped) Boehr was born 11th May 1870 (thus certainly conceived and possibly born out of wedlock) On 10th November 1874 he is admitted to Stockwell College, Lambeth, aged 4. This college opened in 1861 and closed in 1936. It was the British and Foreign School Society's training college for mistresses and had practising schools attached. Age 4 is very young for admittance to a school and this may have been a special needs school. In 1910 he appears in the US census living in Massachusetts, single, age 40, having immigrated in 1895, aged 25. He returned to England because he is then recorded aboard the S.S.Arabic sailing from Liverpool to Boston arriving 8th February 1913. In 1931, age 61, he is in McNeil Island Penitentiary, Washington. His offence is unreadable in the records but is something to do with a service station.

- There was also an Albert George Lawrence Boehr who was born in 1872, baptised in Lambeth and died in 1880.

- Frances Sophia (8, thus born 1873) – in 1918 and 1919 she is on the electoral roll in Battersea.

- Rosalia (6, born December 1874) Mary Frances Rosalia (now dropped in favour of an anglicised name)

- Violetta(4, born 1876) Later she is shown as Christina B. **V.** Boehr. She died in September 1939, aged 63.

- Lilian(3, born 1878) – Ethel Dora Lilian Boehr married William Algernon Thomas Rowe on 19th February 1916 at Wandsworth, she was 38, he was 35.

Then, in later censuses further children appear

- Johanna Clara M. Boehr born September 1881 in Lewisham. In June 1919 she married Edmonds in Wandsworth

- Cecil Rudolph Boehr born December 1896 in Lewisham

- Finally a Hermann Rudolph Boehr married in Lewisham in 1893. He didn't show up earlier and could have been their first born.

The Boehr family seem to have spent most if not all their married life in south London in Lewisham, Wandsworth (he is on the electoral roll in 1894) Battersea and Lambeth. They will have been renting properties and presumably moving as their family got larger and more space was needed. Then, in 1901 they came to 5 Queens Gardens and were the first occupants of our house. Why? Having spent all their lives in south London, why take this big step north? It will not have been in order to have a large house; all but one of their children will have left home by then. It can only be because it was very cheap as compensation for everything going on around. They stayed until 1906 but do not appear on the Ealing electoral roll which suggests they did not regard this as a long term move.

In London, and probably all large cities, one way in which we deal with the scale of the place is by creating suburbs, even villages, within the metropolis. Thus one comes from Ealing not west London. Similarly there are people who have always lived south of the river and would not dream of living north of it, and vice versa, and east and west. For Albert Boehr to leave south London which he will have known so well, a highly developed suburb, for an underdeveloped area north of the river will have been a big and risky move and in 1901 they were in their mid-50s. And one also wonders how Richards and Boehr found each other, did TR put out the word in his club amongst his boss friends that he was looking for a poor but honest clerk to do some house sitting until the property was saleable? To demonstrate how underdeveloped north Ealing was the picture below, taken in 1900, is along Scotch Common, which would become Pitshanger Lane, this was just a year before the Boehrs moved in.

Picture courtesy of Ealing Library

We have seen in the previous chapter that Thomas Richards sold his leasehold to Frank Handover in 1906 and the possible reasons for this. If this was the accommodation of a friend that I suspect then Handover will have had assurances of being made whole but still a free hand to try and improve the returns from the property and so it is quite likely, as the road is nearing completion, that the rent is increased to a level too much for the Boehrs especially as most of their family had now left home and they didn't need such a large house. The next tenant of the house is covered in the next chapter but, first, let's see what the Boehrs did.

And the answer is that they returned to south London. From 1908 to 1911 Albert Boehr was on the electoral roll in Clapham and then in 1911 Albert, aged 65 and Frances Sophia, aged 71, are living at 13 Ravenslea Road, Wandsworth Common and he is noted as a "Woollen Cloth buyer" There are no children noted in the census even though Cecil, above, is only 15. And then in 1918/19 they are in Battersea.

Albert Boehr died in 1921, aged 76. Frances Sophia Boehr died in Wandsworth, Surrey (then) 20th December 1928, aged 88.

What then do we make of Albert Boehr? As manager of the Civil Service S.A (whatever that stands for) and then later a Woollen Cloth buyer he was presumably a modestly prosperous white collar worker who had a large, and occasionally difficult, family to support. None of the office workers in the picture below is Albert Boehr but this is how office workers looked in 1900. Their stay in Queens Gardens may well have been regularly interrupted by builder's traffic but there will have been the compensations described in earlier chapters; indeed it may well have been quite surreal viewing the Benedictine monks to the south in their black outfits, the golfers to the west in their similarly strange attire, the goings on at St Mary's to the north and the artisans to the east; all within less than a mile of the house.

The short period that the Boehrs were in residence was a relatively peaceful time nationally with the major event being the death of Queen Victoria on January 22nd 1901. She was succeeded by her son Edward VII who reigned until 1910. Our House is Victorian in style and was conceived during the Victorian era but technically therefore is Edwardian since it would have been towards the end of 1901 that it was finished. The biggest domestic development was the birth of the Labour Party and the biggest overseas conflict for the British was the second Boer war of 1899 – 1902 (were the Boehrs the butt of jokes about this?) Other events during the Boehr's tenancy were that in 1901 Picasso, aged 19, had his breakthrough exhibition in Paris that launched a glittering career, in 1902 Lenin lived in London for a year, in 1904 number plates were introduced as cars were licensed for the first time, but subject to a speed limit of 20 mph, and in 1905 the Ancient Order of Druids initiated their first rituals at Stonehenge. Also in 1905 another German, an unknown 26 year old working in the Swiss patent office in Bern published a series of papers that became known as Einstien's theory of relativity. Albert Boehr may well have been proud of his fellow countryman's achievement although it took the scientific community many years to fully appreciate Einstein's overturning of Newtonian physics and it may have been decades before the Daily Mail (founded in 1896, just before our house) covered it. And in 1906 the Bakerloo and Piccadilly lines opened on the London Underground.

The Prime Minister was Robert Cecil, Marquess of Salisbury, the last Prime Minister to sit in the House of Lords. He was succeeded in 1902 as head of the Unionist government, by his nephew, Arthur Balfour, who, conveniently for this story, remained in office for the duration of Albert Boehr's tenancy. Today these are all names we may remember from history lessons, but for our house, and its occupants, they were real people who they would have known much about.

Office workers in 1900

We turn now to the House's second tenant and Frank Handover's first.

Chapter 13: Frank Handover & John Richmond 1906-10

By 1906 Queens Gardens was beginning to settle down and become more habitable. The Richards houses in Queens Gardens/ Walk are mostly built. There is building further down Queens Gardens but this is far enough away to be less of a nuisance; by 1908 the road is numbers 1 to 27 (the Richards houses of 1 to 17 have all been built and further building is taking place) by 1910 it is 1 to 29, and by 1912 it is complete at 1 to 41.

But the big change is in the building of the Brentham estate. The map below shows the dates when land was purchased for the development of the estate (building will have started very soon after purchase) The broken lines at the bottom of the map show Queens Gardens. The first areas of the estate to be developed are the darkly shaded ones marked 1901-1905. The road parallel to Queens Gardens is Pitshanger Lane. But in 1901 this did not exist, it was all fields (the map is dated 1911) This shows that the only access for this early Brentham building was along Queens Gardens. But by 1906, or very soon after, Pitshanger Lane was surfaced and the Brentham building spread out and probably no longer used Queens Gardens. Pitshanger Lane as a shopping centre was just starting to develop; the first shop, the Co-op opened in 1906 and by 1908 others would follow (this is in the part of Pitshanger Lane heading from the old farmhouse westwards, off this map) But at least the first 5 years of endless horses and carts and workmen and banging and dust were coming to an end.

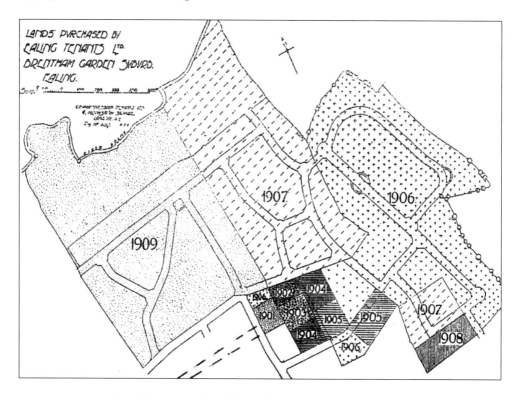

One can only assume that Thomas Richards' application predated the Brentham one or perhaps he underestimated the impact they would have on his plans. TR will have incurred the cost of paving Queens Gardens only to find he was making a free access road for Henry Vivian. Richards and Vivian must have known each other, their developments being in such close proximity. They must surely have hated each other. Even though they were from similarly modest backgrounds HV was a Fabian socialist trying to help workers and TR was a nouveau riche professional pandering to the needs of the middle classes. On top of all this HV was costing TR money because he couldn't sell his houses and had to install a house sitter until things calmed down.

As we have seen on 7th June 1906 TR and the Boatmans Institute assign the lease for our house to Frank Handover for £600 and we have speculated on his motivation in doing this. In 1907 there is no record of an occupant but by 1908 there is a new tenant, John Richmond, and he stays for 2 or 3 years; one assumes that things have improved sufficiently to justify a higher rent than Albert Boehr could afford but not yet enough to consider selling the property.

Frank Handover and John Richmond demonstrate perfectly the challenges of this type of research. It should be possible to find out quite a lot about the former, with his unusual name, but very little about the latter with his rather common one.

In fact it was not quite that simple. There turned out to be two Frank Handovers born within three years of each other (a quite normal margin for error in the records) and both living close to each other in Paddington at one time. They must have been related; probably cousins. The wrong one was Frank *Herbert* Handover, born in 1878 and died in 1958 in Hammersmith. His family lived in Paddington and he was the son of a plumber. In 1901 he is still living at home with his mother, Alice, and he is now a plumber but "own account" meaning self-employed or perhaps with his own business. By 1911 he is 34 and married to Martha May who is 39 and they have 2 sons. They also have a cousin, Reginald George Handover staying with them as well as a visitor, Edith Lee, 26 and a drapery assistant from New York. They are all at 3 High Road, Chiswick. He still describes himself as a plumber but is now definitely an "employer" The right one was Frank *William* Handover, born 1881. In the 1911 census he is 29 and recorded as living at 3 Oxford Gardens, Notting Hill, Paddington. The residence is the property of his in-laws James and Elizabeth Holloway, both 63. Also living there were his wife, Rose Mary Handover, her sister, Annie Holloway, their son, Gordon Handover, 2 boarders (including Adriano Nicol "foreign correspondent") and a domestic servant. James Holloway's profession is "Boarding House keeper" and Frank Handover's is Architects Assistant for an Architect and Surveyor. Frank Handover married in July 1907 and died January 1953 in Plymouth.

We have seen how he bought our house at an inflated price in 1906 but in that year Frank William Handover was only 24 years of age and if he was an architect's assistant in 1911 he was scarcely a surveyor in 1906. He must have been helped in this, perhaps by his father-in-law, perhaps as an inducement to marry his daughter which he did one year later. To buy the property he took a £500 mortgage and paid the £100 balance in cash. At 24 he would surely not have had the equivalent of £100,000 in savings. The connection with TR therefore must surely have been through James Holloway, Boarding House keeper. In such an occupation, and with Franks developing surveying skills and contacts, they will surely have known the value of properties and not unwittingly overpaid and so this purchase must have been a favour to Thomas Richards. As we have seen, in 1910, just 4 years later, the property is sold for £490, realising a loss of £110 or £110,000. For whoever bore this loss it will have been painful.

There is another possible interpretation. Perhaps Frank, helped by his father-in-law-to-be (who had the property opportunity because he was helping TR) thought, as men do, between themselves, that this could be a really good surprise for his wife-to-be. But when she saw it she was horrified "I'm not going to live in a building site stuck in the middle of the countryside with no shops, no way, you'll have to get rid of it!" And so perhaps Frank was stuck with the house until he could dispose of it either at his, or his father-in-law's or TR's expense.

Having bought the lease Handover changed the tenant and installed John Richmond. He appears in the 1909 electoral roll for 5 Queens Gardens but very little else can be found for certain. It is possible he was born in 1868 and was thus 38 when he moved in and it is also possible that he died in 1952, aged 90. If this is the correct person, and the only supporting evidence is that this John Richmond died in Ealing, then he was born in Clerkenwell, the son of a cabinet maker. In 1891 he is living in Wandsworth with his widowed mother who is a matchbox maker and he is listed as a labourer. After his residence in our house in 1911 he is living in Wandsworth married to Maud with 5 children and he is a carpenter. Some of their children will have been born while they were living in our house. It seems likely that he is another convenience tenant like Albert Boehr, installed at a low rent until the area settled down and even, perhaps, as a carpenter, working on some of the houses. But I must stress that much of this is my speculation.

The 1909 electoral roll, however, was interesting for other reasons. By 1909 Pitshanger Lane is much developed with shops appearing. And in Queens Gardens the Richards houses (2 of which are unoccupied) have been joined by 4 more houses (but now semidetached and in a different style) on the same side of the road and the first on the other side of the road.

John Richmond's tenancy was a short one as Frank Handover sold his lease in 1910. The picture below is dated March 1906; was John Richmond either the cyclist or the pedestrian or perhaps working the horse and cart behind? The view is looking into Castlebar Road from Carlton Road and features a tree which will be known to all residents of this part of Ealing; a large tree that is right in the middle of the road. It is still there to this day although much larger now and is effectively a living roundabout. It must have been in a field corner before, perhaps someone's favourite tree, and has miraculously survived to this day.

CASTLEBAR ROAD, EALING.

Frank Handover sold his lease to William Burnham, retired bank clerk of 9 Queens Gardens. Burnham financed this by a mortgage of £470, paying the £20 balance in cash. In the 1909 electoral roll 9 Queens Gardens is occupied by Wilmer Harris Beal and so it would appear that William Burnham bought both number 9 and number 5 in 1910. Not bad for a retired bank clerk. For the next 17 years William Burnham rented out our house; it was not until 1927 that it would become owner occupied. It had, in effect, been an investment plaything for its first 26 years, a successful one for some and not so for others.

The period from 1906 to 1910 was a busy one. Edward VII was on the throne until 1910 and the government, following a landslide general election in 1906 was a Liberal one led by Henry Campbell-Bannerman and then later by Herbert Asquith. There were a number of eminent births in 1907; W. H. Auden, Daphne du Maurier, Lawrence Olivier, Frank Whittle and Peggy Ashcroft. In 1908 Baden Powell published "Scouting for boys" and the Olympics were held in London. They had been scheduled for Rome but an eruption from Vesuvius devastated Naples and a last minute switch was made. It was at these Olympics that the modern distance for the marathon was established. It had previously been 25 miles. However to accommodate the Royal family who wished to see it start from Windsor Castle and end at Buckingham Palace, which was 26 miles 385 yards, a new distance was created where it has remained ever since. In 1909 a State pension scheme starts and Selfridges opened in London as well as the first Woolworths store in Liverpool. In 1910 the London Palladium opened and Dr Crippen poisoned his wife and was later hanged.

Although it was only 4 years away to the ordinary person in the street there was, as yet, no hint of the conflagration that would be the First World War

And so we now turn to the Burnham years.

Chapter 14: William Burnham & Frank George Herbert Alexander Cantopher 1910-17

As we saw in the previous chapter Frank Handover sold his lease to William Burnham, retired bank clerk of 9 Queens Gardens. Burnham financed this by a mortgage of £470, paying the £20 balance in cash. In the 1909 electoral roll 9 Queens Gardens is occupied by Wilmer Harris Beal and so it would appear that William Burnham bought both number 9 and number 5 in 1910. Not bad for a retired bank clerk. For the next 17 years William Burnham rented out our house; it was not until 1927 that it would become owner occupied. It had, in effect, been an investment plaything for its first 26 years, a successful one for some and not so for others. For the first 7 years of his ownership Burnham rented the property to Frank George Herbert Cantopher, the subject of this chapter. Then his next tenant was John Robert Lehmann who was there for the next 10 years and is the subject of the next chapter.

William Burnham was born in 1850 in Maidenhead and he is described in the census as a retired bank cashier. This could mean that he was simply the cashier of a branch bank. But he appears to have been quite wealthy and may have been the head office cashier of one of the major clearing banks. His wife was Maria from Hampton Wick. They had one child, William, born in 1883 in St John's Wood, and in 1901 they were living in Hampstead and he was retired then, aged just 51. In 1910, aged 60 and at least 10 years retired, he bought 9 Queens Gardens, probably with cash, as well as number 5 with a mortgage. One wonders why they chose Ealing for their retirement. It is probably because it was now a settled area but also in the middle of the countryside, as the pictures below show.

By 1910 all of the Thomas Richards houses had been built and the road was nearing completion. Of the 9 Richards houses, numbers 1-17, Thomas Richards still owned all except numbers 5 and 9. If this was the same for Queens Walk and Lyncroft Gardens then he still had enormous debts. He must have been hoping for a quicker turnaround than this. His problem was that home ownership was still relatively uncommon at the time. Only about 20% of properties were owner occupied. It would not be until after 1918 that mortgage finance became more widely available and now owner occupation is 70%

William Burnham died on the 8th September 1920. He had made a will on the 8th November 1900 leaving everything to his wife Maria Ann Burnham. On the 16th March 1921 letters of administration with the will annexed granted the estate to William Lionel Burnham, the son, for the use and benefit of Maria Ann Burnham until she should become of sound mind. She died on the 16th December 1925, intestate (presumably never having regained sound mind) and so the properties passed to the son and only next of kin on 23rd January 1926 and number 5 was then sold by him for £1100 (for the 73 year balance of the lease) on 5th September 1927. The seller is noted as William Lionel Burnham of Broomhill, Boundary road, Carshalton (schoolmaster) and the purchaser was Edward Arthur Fitzgerald of 20 Barnfield road, Ealing (civil servant) who we will come to in a later chapter.

Burnham's first tenant when he bought the property in 1910 was Frank George Herbert Alexander Cantopher and by 1910 the area was much more congenial, indeed our house achieved the ultimate in gentrification, a name "Rockcliffe" as well as a number, 5. There was no such sign when we bought the house but the name is in the Kelly's directories for 1910 and 1911 and our next door neighbours in number 7 still have their original name, Gresham Lodge. Were the names a way of distancing themselves from the noisy artisans of the Brentham estate just down the road and perhaps allying themselves with the grand and named, large houses in the neighbourhood? The only source I can think of for the name relates to the first tenant whose family for a while lived in Glasgow and Rockcliffe (pictured below) is a beautiful coastal village in Dumfries and Galloway about 50 miles from the city. Did William Burnham ask Frank Cantopher for suggestions for a name and he picked the place where his family had had their summer holidays?

Frank Cantopher (hereafter we will make him George since he drops Frank in all official records) was born on 16th December 1882 at Berhampur, Bengal, India. He was the son of Bernard William Cantopher, a civil engineer, and Mariquita Engracia M L Guibara. He married firstly Katherine Evelyn Keily, daughter of Edward William Keily and Helena Maria Bourke, on 11th

August 1908 at the Church of the Faithful Virgin, Upper Norwood, Surrey. He married secondly Betty Capon on 4th May 1946 at London. He died on 1st February 1966 at Ningwood, Isle of Wight, aged 83. With his first wife he had four children; Mary Joy (born 19 April 1912, died 1st September 1913) Elizabeth Mary (born 26th December 1913, died 6th April 1990) Peter George Alexander (born 4th December 1915, died 17th November 1971) and Richard Bernard Alexander (born 18th February 1917, died 11th February 21 1970)

In the 1901 census he is living at 43 Farquhar Road, Camberwell, a batchelor, aged 19. He has just moved down from Glasgow where his family were noted as Mariquita Cantopher, his mother and "head" (his father has presumably died, or perhaps is absent, overseas) aged 44 and born in Glasgow, Georgina Guibara, his grandmother, aged 78 and born in Sunderland, his brother William Joseph Cantopher, aged 19 and born in Bombay, India, his sister, Hilda, aged 10 and born in Glasgow and another sister Sybil, aged 8 and born in Burmah, Pegu. George himself is recorded as a mercantile clerk born in Bengal, India. This was clearly a highly colonial family that had moved extensively around the world. Indeed the name Cantopher itself is quite exotic, being of Belgian origin and an Anglicisation of Kant, meaning border, and fort meaning the same in English.

In 1910 George moved into our house along with his new wife (of 2 years) his mother, his three sisters and a servant. Gradually he started his own family and children start to come along, in 1913, then 1915 and finally in 1917. Ours is a reasonably large house but this must have been quite a squash and the last child, Richard Bernard Alexander in 1917, as well as the others growing up, must have been the reason they terminated their tenancy in that year to find a yet larger house. In fact they didn't move far, just to 21 Blakesley Avenue, for about 7 years, pictured below, and then to 19 Hertford Street, W1, his business clearly having prospered, pictured immediately after. 21 Blakesley Avenue today has been turned into flats and is a little rundown. 100 years ago it will have been a grand house as still is 19 Hertford Street which follows. It is located about 100 yards from St Benedicts Abbey.

19 Hertford Street is in Mayfair just behind the Hilton hotel. As well as being his family home this must have also been used for his business as well. His business, as we shall see, was rice. Today the above property is the Mayfair Islamic centre. It is intriguing that George will have travelled East from this base in pursuit of his trade, West meets East, and now the reverse has happened as East meets West.

George's profession is described as "Merchant, Burma Rice Trade" Burma (now Myanmar) was a British colony (actually a province of India) from 1886 until independence in 1948. During British rule the country prospered (or at least the colonists did) and it became the world's largest exporter of rice. The London Rice Brokers Association was formed in 1870 to regularise trading and George is likely to have been a member. From the above property he clearly prospered.

The rice trade at the time was variously described as either "The Devil's business" or "The Grand National of Commerce" It was, apparently, a trade marked by chiselling competition and wildly fluctuating price levels. For most of the colonial period most of Burma's rice was exported to Britain, and then about half was re-exported to Europe, and its uses were mainly for making alcohol, starch and for animal feed; not, until later, for human consumption. In 1870 545 ships carried 396,358 tons of rice; in 1910, 579 much larger ships carried 1,521,181 tons. This was George's trade and he shows up about twice a year in the shipping lists travelling out to Burma as well as North America, sometimes with his wife and family.

Ealing was popular with colonial families at this time, either retired colonials that have come home or, such as George, traders in the colonies. For younger families the availability of good schools will have been important; for retired families the semi-rural atmosphere that we have noted may well have been attractive. Agatha Christie wrote in her memoirs:

'Ealing at that time had the same characteristics as Cheltenham or Leamington Spa. The retired military and navy came there in large quantities for the 'healthy air' and the advantage of living so near London. Grannie led a thoroughly social life – she was a sociable woman at all times. Her house was always full of old Colonels and Generals for whom, she would embroider waistcoats and knit bed socks...Their gallantry always made me feel rather shy. The jokes they cracked for my amusement did not seem funny, and their arch, rallying manner made me nervous'.

It is worth recalling that in the nineteenth century, the most important part of the British Empire was India, as it was until independence in 1947. The 1921 census abstract for Ealing notes that there were 743 residents born in India who were also described as 'European'. It must have seemed a natural place for George Cantopher to bring his family.

George retired to Ryde on the Isle of Wight. He and his first wife are buried in Ryde Cemetery and their inscriptions read, on the south side, "In your charity pray for the repose of the soul of Katherine Evelyn (Kitty) Cantopher nee Keily, born Nov 2nd 1880, died 19th 1944" and on the north side "And of her husband George Herbert Alexander Cantopher born Dec 16th 1882 died Feb 1st 1966" and on the west side "In memory of great unselfish love"

His probate in 1966 amounted to £9680. In 1966 the average wage was £20 per week or £1000 pa. The average equivalents today are 20 times larger making his estate about £200,000 in today's values. But with at least 3 children he may well have bequeathed much more to them before he died since by 1966 estate taxation was well in place.

The period of George's tenancy in our house, 1910 to 1917, was a fairly turbulent one nationally and internationally. In 1911 there was a revolution in China resulting in the overthrow of the Qing Dynasty (did this disrupt his business in Burma?) In 1912 the Titanic sank, and on June 4th 1913 Emily Wilding Davison flung herself in front of the King's horse at the Derby, but it would not be until 1928 that women finally did get the vote. 1914 saw the outbreak of World War 1, which we will return to, 1916 saw the Easter rising in Ireland and 1917 saw the two Russian revolutions, in March and then again in October. On a more positive note in 1911 Ernest Rutherford discovered the structure of the atom. These events, which we were taught about in history lessons at school, have occurred within the lifetime of Our House, and its occupants, who probably read about them in the daily newspapers and many of them would have far reaching consequences to this very day. Such is history, and we are just a suburban house not Windsor Castle.

Constitutionally Edward VII died in 1910 and George V assumed the throne and Asquith was Prime Minister from 1908 to 1916 and was then replaced by David Lloyd George who governed until 1922. But the key event was, of course, World War 1.

Ealing's contribution in this conflict was probably not much different to that of any other town (except perhaps for the many retired military types residing locally; were any remobilised or at least called for advice?) Men enlisted either in the Middlesex regiment, the Royal Fusiliers or the London regiment. 1058 Ealing residents died in the war and are commemorated in the memorial below outside Pitshanger Manor in the centre of Ealing.

George Cantopher did not enlist, presumably being deemed engaged in important work for the war effort. There was a limited amount of bombing of London but there was no bomb damage in Ealing, most of the Zeppelin raids were to central and east London. The nearest to Ealing was when a bomb fell on Brentford and Ealing residents visited the bomb site as a curiosity. Air raids consisted of bombs being erratically lobbed from Zeppelin balloons. It would only be 20 years (the time it took digital phones to evolve from 1st generation to the current technology) before it became much more serious.

Since 1921 World War 2 casualties have been added to the memorial and there is a dedication which reads as follows;

They come transfigured back
Secure from change
In their high hearted ways
Beautiful evermore
And with the rays
Of morn on their white
Shields of expectation

It is difficult to decide if this is municipal doggerel, albeit with the best intentions; it would certainly not seem applicable to the second World War even if it was applicable to the first.

This chapter concludes with a couple of World War 1 pictures simply to give a flavour of the times. The first is an unknown regiment, the second is also unknown but does show central London in 1914 and the third is the Middlesex regiment itself on manoeuvres.

And so we move on to the second of William Burnham's tenants, John Robert Lehmann who occupied our house from 1917 to 1927.

Chapter 15: John Robert Lehmann 1917-27

John Robert Lehmann was born in 1892 in Ealing. He was part of a large and prosperous family. There were 11 children and the first 5 were daughters. In the 1901 (and 1911) census the family are living at Moorside, Somerset Road, Ealing. The head of the family is Robert Lehmann, aged 54, a condensed milk merchant, working for himself. He is a Swiss subject born in Lausanne. The rest of the family are his wife, Marie (55 in 1901) Jeanne (27) Marie (21) Suzanne (20) Emma (20, twins?) Helene Julia (19) and Edward (18) and all of these were born in Switzerland and are recorded as Swiss nationals; then, born in England but still recorded as Swiss nationals were Henry David (16) Marguerite (15) Ernest Paul (13) and Alice Henriette (12). Then, last of all, along comes John Robert (9 in 1901) the only member of the family who is not a Swiss subject. Roughly half their family were born in Lausanne and the other half in Ealing. In an amusing parallel the writer's family also splits half and half but on a much smaller scale. Our daughter was born in Ealing and our son in Geneva (just down the road from Lausanne) Moorside, Somerset Road, Ealing is pictured below.

As we shall see the Lehmanns were a wealthy family and whilst their original home is now barely visible in this overdeveloped and gated collection of flats it clearly was a substantial property and the gables give a slightly Swiss appearance which may have appealed to them.

Since Edward was born in Switzerland in 1883 and Henry was born in Ealing in 1885, the family immigrated sometime between these 2 dates. There were no wars or revolutions in Switzerland in the 1880s that might explain their emigration but Switzerland then was not the wealthy country it is now. Population growth and famine forced hundreds of thousands of Swiss to emigrate during the 19th century. In particular there were waves of emigration in 1816-7, 1845-55 and 1880-85 and many of these went to North America. But the Lehmanns were a rich family and their emigration may well have been because England offered greater commercial opportunities in condensed milk and starch, which we will come to in a moment.

In the 1901 census they had 3 servants as well as a Swiss nephew and a Swiss visitor staying with them. In the 1911 census Marie is now a widow living on "private means" Henry is an assistant manager and condensed milk and starch merchant, Ernest is a branch manager and John Robert is an engineering student. They still have 3 servants. As we will see later it is likely that all the male offspring worked in their father's speciality of condensed milk and starch.

Condensed milk is cow's milk from which water has been removed. It is most often found in the form of sweetened condensed milk, with sugar added, and the two terms 'condensed milk' and 'sweetened condensed milk' are often used synonymously today. Sweetened condensed milk is a very thick, sweet product which when canned can last for years without refrigeration if unopened. Though there have been unsweetened condensed milk products, they spoiled far more easily and are uncommon nowadays. Condensed milk is used in numerous dessert dishes in many countries.

The U.S. government ordered huge amounts of it as a field ration for Union soldiers during the American Civil War. This was an extraordinary field ration for the 19th century: a typical 10 ounce (300 ml) can contained 1,300 Calories, 1 ounce each of protein and fat, and more than 7 ounces of carbohydrate.

Soldiers returning home from the Civil War soon spread the word. By the late 1860s, condensed milk was a major product. The first Canadian factory was built at Truro, Nova Scotia, in 1871 and in 1899, E. B. Stuart opened the first Pacific Coast Condensed Milk Company (later known as the Carnation Milk Products Company) plant in Kent, Washington. In 1911, Nestlé constructed the world's largest condensed milk plant in Dennington, Victoria, Australia. Nestlé's headquarters, then and now, are in Vevey, which is close to Lausanne. Is this where Robert Lehmann (John's father) picked up his interest in the product? Perhaps he worked for Nestlé and was sent by them to London to develop the market or perhaps to oversee the import of milk from the USA.

Starch is a carbohydrate consisting of a large number of glucose units joined by glycosidic bonds. This polysaccharide is produced by all green plants as an energy store. It is the most common carbohydrate in the human diet and is contained in large amounts in such staple foods as potatoes, wheat, maize, rice, and cassava.

Pure starch is a white, tasteless and odourless powder that is insoluble in cold water or alcohol. Starch is processed to produce many of the sugars in processed foods. Dissolving starch in warm water gives wheat paste, which can be used as a thickening, stiffening or gluing agent. The biggest industrial non-food use of starch is as adhesive in the papermaking process. Starch can be applied to parts of some garments before ironing, to stiffen them; this is less usual now than in the past.

In 1932 the passenger list for Cunard's Asconia sailing from Montreal to Quebec, Le Havre and Plymouth recorded John Lehmann (age 40) and his brother Henry (46) both of Mattock Lane, Ealing, and both "merchants" as well as Charles Lehmann (59 of Woldingham House, Woldingham) his wife Jane (57) and daughter, Phyllis (27) These are clearly relatives because they are all in the same suite and so it is possible an entire extended family emigrated in the 1890s (there is also a record of an Otto Lehmann born in 1877 who died in Ealing in 1952 and an Albert Lehmann born 1887 and died in Ealing in 1959)

Note also that John Lehmann is now a "merchant" having previously been an engineering student. It would seem that he and his brother Henry have taken over their father's condensed milk and starch business and this, perhaps, is the reason they have travelled to North America. John Lehmann and various other Lehmanns appear regularly in the passenger lists (no sooner had he returned from the above trip, which left Montreal on 19th June 1932 than he set off from Southampton to New York on 26th July aboard Cunard's Franconia barely a month later) If there had been "sea miles" in those days he would have done well.

John Lehmann was 18 when his father died and his brother, Ernest, was 22 so they were quite old enough to take over the business and the First World War must have been very profitable for them. Their father, Robert Arthur Lehmann, died in March 1903, he was just 56. His executors were his widow, Marie Louise and a Charles Theodore Lehmann, merchant, presumably a brother, and he left a staggering £55,312 16s and 1d, equivalent by our ready reckoner, to £55 million in today's money. If he wasn't rich when he immigrated then he certainly became so having arrived. Condensed milk and starch was clearly a good trade to be in.

John Robert Lehmann married Barbara Cole in 1914 in Brentford. He was 22 and she was 24. Her family home then was The cottage, The Green, Elers road, Ealing and her father was Thomas Cole "artist and art master, science and art department" Elers Road is barely a hundred yards from the Lehmann property in Somerset Road and it could be that the families knew each other and perhaps John and Barbara played together as children in nearby Lammas Park. Today there is no green in Elers Road only a block of modern flats in amongst the Victorian villas which is where it probably was. The Cole family only had 1 servant and they moved later to 17 Mattock Lane. In 1917 John and Barbara moved into our house and they lived there for 10 years until 1927 when they moved to 17 Mattock Lane which is pictured below and which had been occupied by the Cole family. In 1925 whilst living in Our House the telephone number was Ealing 1497. When they moved to Mattock Lane they kept the same number. They moved from our house because it was being sold, as we have seen, and the purchaser was buying it for his own occupation.

17 Mattock Lane

John Robert died in June 1959, aged 67. Barbara continued to live at Mattock Lane until her death in 1973, aged 84. I have not been able to trace any children definitively but there was a John R Lehmann living with Barbara in 1962 so it is assumed this is a son with his father's name and there was also an R P Lehmann in the telephone directory for 1973 living at 35 Mattock Lane.

The executors for John Robert's will were his widow and Richard Paul Lehmann, presumably a cousin or uncle or a son, and his estate was £9,646 8s 8d. This would be plenty for his widow to live on but is surprisingly small considering the wealth of his father and the apparent prosperity of his business.

What are we to conclude about their lives on, admittedly, very little information? He came from a very rich immigrant family and must have inherited a trade from his father that must make their fortune. She came from a lower middle class (only 1 servant!) and perhaps slightly bohemian background. After Our House they moved into her parents' house and stayed there for the rest of their lives, 32 years for him and 46 for her. And despite coming from large families, especially him, they appear to have had only 1 or 2 children at most. But, above all, where did family wealth go? There is a Wall Street crash and a Great Depression to come in the 1930s so perhaps it was lost during that time. His brothers, Henry David and Ernest Paul also left modest amounts when they died so it would seem the family fortune just disappeared.

By the time John Lehmann moved from our house the development of North Ealing was more or less complete, all the spaces had been filled in and farming was extinct by 1930. Railway lines, both underground and over ground, were as they are today and North Ealing was a fully functioning suburb.

Constitutionally George V was on the throne for this entire period and the Prime Ministers were Lloyd George (Lib/Coalition) 1916-1920, Andrew Bonar Law (Con) briefly and then Stanley Baldwin (Con) and Ramsay MacDonald (Lab) alternating for most of the next 20 years.

During the period of John Lehmann's residence there were a number of national and international developments that would have important long term consequences.

Following the end of World War 1 in 1918 John Maynard Keynes published "The economic consequences of the peace" arguing that the peace settlement imposed on the defeated countries were too harsh and would create trouble and it was not very long before storm clouds were again brewing everywhere. In 1921 Adolf Hitler became Chairman of the Nazi party in Germany and 4 years later published "Mein Kampf" and in 1921 Mao Tse-Tung founded the Communist party in China. The following year Mussolini came to power in Italy at the head of the Fascist party. As a traveling businessman John Lehmann was probably well aware of these even if the general public were not.

In Britain in 1926 there was a general strike lasting 9 days, a reaction to the post war austerity. This scarcely affected Ealing which had virtually no factories and certainly no coal mining.

In 1920 prohibition was introduced in the USA following the 18th amendment. But, on a brighter note, this year saw the start of BBC daily radio transmissions; the techniques having been proved by Marconi in 1901. It is difficult to underestimate the importance of this, and especially television when it followed. Adult literacy was still low in 1920 and the BBC filled this gap. In 1924 Rhapsody in Blue was penned by George Gershwin and IBM was founded, John Logie Baird invented the first television transmitter and Margaret Thatcher was born. Round about this time the fashions of the day were as below.

Ealing is often described as being multicultural as if that is a modern phenomenon. But the history of our house shows that this has been the case for a long time. Our first resident was a Prussian/Polish refugee orphan, the second an Englishman, the third a Scottish/Belgian born in India and the fourth a part of a Swiss family. Let us see what comes next.

Chapter 16: Edward Arthur Fitzgerald 1927-40

In answer to the rhetorical question that closed the last chapter the answer is that the next occupiers were Irish, or, at least, of Irish descent. Edward Arthur Fitzgerald was born in Cornwall but he was part of a very Irish family. His parents, William and Annie, were both born in Dublin in 1850. They appear to have moved around frequently seeking work. After Edward was born in Cornwall in 1877, his two younger sisters were born in Ireland and he had a younger brother, Denis, who was born in Liverpool. By 1881 the family are in 58 Queen Street, Shrewsbury and William is working in the Excise office. By 1891 they are in Birkenhead and William is a sanitary inspector and they have another daughter, Elizabeth, who was born in Ireland. They have been criss crossing the Irish Sea on a regular basis. This may well have been due to the Irish potato famine of 1845-1852 following which economic conditions in Ireland were very difficult for many years. But things may well have been looking up because in 1891 they have a servant and a lodger. By 1901 they are still in Birkenhead but William is now a District Sanitary Inspector. By 1911 Annie is a widow living with her son, Denis, and so William has died very young.

But it is their son, Edward Arthur Fitzgerald who bought our house. He was born in 1877 in Chasewater (pictured below) which is 3 miles from Redruth and 5 miles from Truro. The only work for his father in this tiny village would have been either mining or farming. It was a short lived tenure because by 1881 (above) they are in Shrewsbury.

He will have accompanied his family on all their travels and first appears on his own in 1911 living at 6 Riverview Grove, Chiswick, with his wife, Amelia Marie (born 1880 in Arundel) they had married in 1908, and the first of their surviving children (one died in childbirth) Mary Doreen aged 7 months, as well as a boarder, Louisa Shea, 67 years old and single. He is a clerk working for the GPO and so they seem to have a more stable existence than his parents did. Indeed when they moved into our house in 1927 Edward and Amelia lived there for the rest of their lives and their 2 daughters for most of theirs. Edward died in 1940, aged 63 but Amelia survived until 1971, aged 91. In this chapter I will thus cover the period 1927 until Edward's death in 1940, and the next chapter will cover 1940 until the house is sold in 1972.

On 5th September 1927 there was an assignment of 5 Queens Gardens from William Lionel Burnham (realising the estate of his parents) to Edward Arthur Fitzgerald of 20 Barnfield Road, civil servant, for £1100. The house was now 26 years old and the first owner occupier was about to move in; which shows that buy-to-let is not such a modern phenomenon. Although described as a civil servant Edward might still have been employed by the GPO since it was a nationalised company in those days.

Edward Fitzgerald and his family did not have far to move. 20 Barnfield Road (pictured above) is barely 400 yards from our house. Barnfield Road will have derived its name from the Pitshanger farmhouse since the road joins Pitshanger Lane where the western end would have been and where, presumably, the farm's barn stood. It is a Brentham estate house. As we shall see the

Fitzgeralds did not have a large family and presumably their reason for moving was a simple desire to join the growing popularity of home ownership. They paid £1100 for the house which compares with the building cost of £600 in 1901, the £600 sale by Thomas Richards to Frank Handover in 1906 and the sale by Handover to William Burnham for £490 in 1910. The value of the house has more than doubled in 17 years.

It is possible that buying our house was a financial stretch for Edward; he was, after all, 50 when he bought it. On 19th January 1934, 7 years after buying the property a legal charge is registered by the Burnley building society and the mortgagor is Edward Arthur Fitzgerald. This consolidates several loans – 25th October 1927 £400 (barely a month after buying the property), 3rd November 1927 £47 9s 4d, 8th June 1928 £114 8s 8d, 20th April 1931 £55.0.0 and 19th January 1934 £60.0.0. He has taken second mortgages equivalent to nearly half the original purchase price. Are they a profligate family or perhaps he lost his job but could not bear to move? In today's terms these are enormous sums, equivalent to about half a million pounds; perhaps he made some ill-advised investments. After he had died in 1940 his widow had to get to grips with all their debts and it was not until the 19th July 1963 that the Burnley Building Society confirmed the receipt of all outstandings and release of the legal charge.

Edward Arthur died 3rd January 1940, he was aged 63 and had only had 13 years in the house, and by his will (dated 20th August 1917) the lease (still in the original name of Sceptre Investment Co and Thomas Richards) vested in his wife, Amelia Marie Theresa Fitzgerald and this was formalised by an assent dated 25th April 1940. His effects, apart from the property, amounted to £366 9s 2d.

Edward and Amelia had at least 2 children, possibly three. The 2 daughters were Mary Doreen and Moira Theresa (often Theresa Moira) Mary was born in July 1910 and died in 1983. Theresa has been harder to track and was certainly born after the 1911 census or she would have shown up in it. The 3rd child is believed to Desmond Joseph Fitzgerald, probably born in 1920 and died 2005.

In this chapter we are dealing with Edward's time in the house, 1927 to 1940, more of the children in the next.

North Ealing in 1927 will not have looked much different to today; most of the housing development was completed and farming was extinct by 1930. Horses were still much in evidence but cars were becoming more common. The Western Avenue (A 40) was upgraded in the 1930s to take the extra traffic. As the area developed schools were needed and in 1931 Notting Hill School for girls was opened and the 1930 picture below shows, on the left, Whinney House School in Eaton Rise. Eaton Rise was the first road to be developed to the immediate north of Haven Green in the 1860s. In 1888 the school was described as"a desirable home for Indian and orphan children" where "Indian" meant children of British parents who lived in India, a theme we have explored before. The picture is of poor quality but it is remarkable how empty the road is of traffic and the delightful dress of the lady walker can just be seen.

Constitutionally George V was the King until his death on 20th January 1936 whereupon his son, Edward VIII became King and caused an almighty problem. He wanted to marry Wallis Simpson, an American divorcee and after much wrangling he abdicated on the 11th December 1936 in favour of his brother, George VI. Politically the period 1927 to 1940 is fairly easy to describe; there were a series of national governments led variously by Ramsay MacDonald, Stanley Baldwin and Neville Chamberlain. Governing will not have been easy. The aftermath of World War 1 was soon followed by the Great Depression (see later) and there was a significant rise of Fascism on the continent but also, to a lesser extent, in this country. The swinging 30s (see later) masked growing storm clouds which soon would burst.

There was some good news however; in 1928 women finally got the vote on the same terms as men. Amelia and her daughters must have been delighted.

Internationally the period until Edward's death in 1940 was incredibly turbulent and eventful. It began badly with the Wall Street crash of 1929 (which was compounded in the USA by dust storms and crop failures) which led to the Great Depression and ended badly with another World War. But in between there was an outpouring of incredible creativity, much of it emanating from the USA, that may well have been an attempt to ignore what was going on. The American cultural influence became more prominent than ever before and heralded the rise of the USA as a superpower. The Fitzgeralds would have listened on their radio to Glenn Miller, Benny Goodman, Bing Crosby, Count Basie, Frank Sinatra, Tommy Dorsey, Louis Armstrong and many others as well as their British counterparts. They might have gone to the cinema to see Clark Gable, Bette Davis, Greta Garbo, Errol Flynn or Fred Astaire or perhaps a Disney movie (Snow White and the seven dwarfs was the first in 1937) or to see Gone with the wind (1939)

But the storm clouds could not be ignored forever. In 1933 Hitler became Chancellor of Germany and when the 1936 Olympics were held in Berlin he made no secret of his intentions. Just 2 years later Hitler annexed Austria and on 1st September 1939 Germany invaded Poland and 2 days later, on Sunday September 3rd Britain and France declared war on Germany. The swinging 30s had come to an end. The impact of the war on Ealing will be examined in the next chapter. But one very remarkable event took place soon after war was declared. Operation Pied Piper had been planned since 1938 and involved the evacuation of all children from London and other cities that might be in the firing line. During 4 days in September over 100,000 children passed through Ealing Broadway station; an incredible logistical exercise.

We turn now to Edward's widow and her family from 1940 to 1972.

Chapter 17: Amelia Marie Fitzgerald 1940-72

After her husband's death Amelia was left with 3 children (albeit grown up) an expensive house to run, a mountain of debts and all this with a World War under way. It will have been a very worrying time. But, as we will see, she succeeded admirably and lived until her 92nd year. To cope with the house and the debts she must have had to get a job although it is likely she already had one since Edward's GPO salary probably was insufficient to afford an expensive house in the first place.

Her three children were Mary Doreen, born July 1910 and died in 1983, Moira Theresa (often Theresa Moira) born in 1913 and Desmond Joseph Fitzgerald, probably born in 1920 and died 2005. Unfortunately it has not been possible to find out very much about any of the children. The most valuable source of definite information is the 10 yearly census. But under the Freedom of Information act these are only publically available 100 years after their collection. Thus Mary Doreen appeared in the 1911 census, aged 7 months, living with her parents at 6 River View, Chiswick, but the others postdate this and Fitzgerald is a common name.

It would seem that they all lived in our house for some of their lives but not necessarily for all. Moira is recorded on local electoral rolls at 120 Kingshill Avenue, Ealing in 1948/9 and later, in 1965, at Tenby gardens. In 1949 Amelia signs a deed for the Burnley Building Society as part of clearing up the debts she is left with and she and Desmond, who stands surety, are recorded as being resident at 5 Queens Gardens. Then Amelia died on 29th December 1971 and on the 4th February 1972 the property passed to Miss Mary Doreen Fitzgerald and Miss Moira Theresa Fitzgerald, both of 5 Queens Gardens. When Amelia died her estate was worth £8750 and this would have excluded the house. It is possible that Amelia left the house to the daughters and the balance of her estate to Desmond.

For whatever reason the sisters did not stay long after their mother had died. On 14th December 1972, barely a year later, searches preparatory to a sale have started on behalf of John Leslie Harlow Kitchin and his wife, Maude Cecile Kitchin. Their mother had lived to 92 years old and must have needed a lot of help and support. The sisters were now in their late 50s or early 60s, they had never married, and perhaps felt that now was the time to start a new life, and this is where we lose track of them.

In later house transactions we will find that on 23rd June 1977 Harrow Land Registry refers to "The Freehold land...registered on 30th April 1965" Thus Amelia acquired the freehold just 7 years before her death, probably helped by her children. As we shall see later this is only 2 years after she finally repaid all the debts left to her by Edward. And so finally Thomas Richards and the Sceptre Investment Company are no longer the head lessors and disappear from the life of our house. The Fitzgerald family had lived in the house for 45 years. By the time they left the house was 71 years old and they had lived in it for 63% of its life.

But we need to return to 1940 and Amelia's predicament following the death of her husband. Edward had died on the 3rd January 1940; 6 months later the Blitz started. This was Germany's attempt to bomb Britain into submission thereby to facilitate Operation Sea Lion, the invasion of the mainland. From 7th September 1940 until 21st April 1941 London was attacked 71 times and 18291 tons of high explosive was dropped on the city. The first bomb on Ealing was on 11th September. At the outset of the assault London was bombed for 57 consecutive nights and more than 1 million homes were destroyed or damaged and 20,000 civilians were killed. Ealing inevitably had its share of this and 563 high explosive bombs and 3 parachute mines were dropped. There were at least 6 bombs within a few hundred yards of our house (3 within 100 yards in Glencairn Drive and Buckingham Close) and approximately 30 bombs were dropped in the square mile covered by this book. 217 people were killed in Ealing.

In this part of London targets would have been RAF Northolt (2 or 3 miles away) and RAF Northwood (5 or 6 miles away) and the Hoover building (now Tesco, less than half a mile away) Hoover had contracts to produce aircraft parts and the building had been painted green in an attempt to camouflage it, although it is a rather large and obvious target. As was said at the time 'as camouflage it was, of course, useless, but as a sign of the times it was conclusive. The Hoover factory had put on battle-dress'.

Other local sites that we have covered were also affected. Ealing Abbey was seriously damaged and the Golf Club was hit. On 15th November 1940 a bomb fell on the clubhouse and 6 people were killed including the Club Steward and his wife and their son, John, who was a choir boy at St Mary's Perivale (see earlier) and had attended church that morning. In fact the golf club also lost 4 holes before the war had even started when in August 1939 an antiaircraft gun site was built, parts of which are still there. This would have been positioned to protect the Hoover building, just the other side of what is now the A40. The site was returned to the club in June 1949. There is also, to this day, a bomb crater by the side of the 11th green.

Close to the golf club and St Mary's church, on the north side of the A40 there was a raid over north Ealing on 25th September 1940, when a parachute mine fell on houses in Medway Drive, killing six people. This led to a royal visit two days later which was reported as follows:

'On Friday the King and Queen, with the mayor and officials in attendance, visited a north west district in the London area, which had been badly damaged by a high explosive bomb the previous Wednesday night. Their Majesties spoke consoling words to those rendered homeless and expressed sympathy with the bereaved. They commanded the mayor to send messages of sympathy to the relatives'.

Close to Medway Drive and only a mile or two from our house was RAF Northolt. A total of 4000 bombs were recorded as falling within two miles of the airfield although only two actually hit it. Northolt was the home of No. 303 the Polish Fighter Squadron, believed to be the highest "scoring" squadron in the RAF. Nearby is the Polish War Memorial.

The Nazi tactic failed; their bombing was not sufficiently accurate to wipe out war time production and it did not dent public morale and Hitler then turned his attention eastwards in Operation Barbarossa, and things settled down in Ealing, for a while.

Later in the war, in 1944, the Germans started launching the V1 flying bomb and the V2 rockets. 9521 of the former were launched and 300 of the latter. The V1 bombs were fairly untargeted and easy to shoot down but the V2 rockets could be deadly although Ealing escaped relatively unscathed. Between June 1944 and March 1945 eleven V1 rockets fell on Ealing. The worst incident was on 21st July. This was when a bomb fell on the Uxbridge Road in West Ealing between Hartington Road and Drayton Green Road. The road was blocked, five shops were destroyed and there was damage to property within a half mile radius. A total of 23 people were killed, six seriously injured and another 148 had minor injuries. The only V2 rocket to fall on the borough was on 6th November, and it exploded in mid-air over central Ealing. Parts of it fell on south Ealing and also on the Mount Park area. In total, the bombing at this time resulted in 53 people dead, 73 were seriously hurt and 382 had lesser injuries. This was far fewer than had been killed in the Blitz.

War ended in 1945. On 8th May was VE day, which saw bonfires in Walpole Park and on Horsenden Hill, thanksgiving services in churches, street parties, flags and ribbons being much in evidence and dancing on Ealing Green. On the 13th there was a service of thanksgiving in Walpole Park, where contingents of the armed forces, Home Guard and civil defence organisations took part. VJ day was 3 months later on August 15th 9 days after "Little Boy" was dropped on Hiroshima.

Cheering crowds in Piccadilly Circus.

And so Amelia and her children survived the war and now had to get on with making a living and repaying their debts. This cannot have been easy. It was not until the 19th July 1963 that the Burnley Building Society confirmed the receipt of all outstandings and the release of their legal charge. Amelia was 83 years of age when finally rid of the debts, her family must have helped.

Constitutionally there is only one change to report for the rest of this book. George VI died on February 6th 1952 at Sandringham, he was only 56. His daughter, Princess Elizabeth, aged 25, thus ascended to the throne, but she was in Kenya. She had left England on 31st January to represent her ailing father on a trip to take in Kenya, Australia and New Zealand. She and the Duke of Edinburgh (who she had married at Westminster Abbey on November 20th 1947) had completed their official duties in Kenya and were resting at the Treetops hotel before the next stage of their trip when the news came through. They immediately returned home and her Coronation took place on June 2nd 1953 at Westminster Abbey. Three days before her coronation, on 29th May 1953, Hillary and Tenzing conquered Everest. It took time for this news to get to

London and the Coronation and the Everest triumph seemed to blend into one. As we shall see there was not much else to be happy about

One effect of the Coronation especially was to boost sales of television sets dramatically. BBC radio transmission had started in 1922 and experimental television transmission started in 1932 with the first proper service being broadcast from Alexandra Palace from November 1936. But the take up was very slow and the service was then suspended for the duration of the war only restarting in June 1946. The take up continued to be slow, picking up a little for the 1948 Olympics in London (these were the austerity Games, no new facilities were built, somewhat different to 2012 when London became the only City to host the Games three times) but then in 1953 everyone wanted to see the Coronation and if you didn't have a set then you found friends who did and television took off.

The BBC also had a direct effect on Ealing. Because so many of the BBC studios and offices were in West London Ealing almost became a BBC ghetto. Many producers, cameramen, presenters and even an ex-Director General lived in Ealing, and particularly north Ealing, and in our road, because of its proximity to their work. They replaced the generals and colonials of earlier chapters.

If you didn't have television there was of course still the cinema and Ealing made a unique contribution to this art form. Ealing studios started in 1902 and it is the oldest continuously working facility for film production in the world. It came into its own in the post war period with many classic films such as *Kind Hearts and Coronets* (1949 Alec Guinness, Joan Greenwood and Dennis Price) *Passport to Pimlico* (1949 Stanley Holloway, Margaret Rutherford and Hermione Baddeley) *The Lavender Hill Mob* (1951 Alec Guinness, Stanley Holloway, Sid James and Alfie Bass) and *The Ladykillers* (1955 Alec Guinness, Peter Sellers and Jack Warner) The studios are still working to this day and more recent productions have been Z Cars, Colditz and The Singing Detective.

But apart from the conquest of Everest and the Coronation Ealing, and the country in general was a dreary and drab place for many years. The war had exhausted and nearly bankrupted the country. London was covered in bomb sites many of which still existed 20 or more years later (although 2 enterprising businessmen, Messrs Hobson and Gosling, built a business, National Car Parks, converting the inner city bomb sites into car parks to serve the ever growing number of cars and eventually sold their business in 1998 for £800 million)

Most houses in Ealing (and elsewhere) had been neglected during the six years of the war as paint and wallpaper were scarce or non-existent from 1939 right up to the 1950s. As a result, buildings in Britain's towns and suburbs looked shabby and badly in need of attention, even those that escaped the bombing. Rationing of food and materials continued long after the war, finally finishing in July 1954. All of this was compounded by a very severe winter in 1947 when coal supplies were very low following the war and when eventually the weather turned the huge snow drifts caused widespread flooding. Then, to follow this, there was a very hot summer and Ealing houses, being built on clay, suffered subsidence everywhere.

But perhaps the worst thing was that the wartime spirit that had held the country together was no longer a unifying force, everyone had to fend for themselves. Of necessity, during the war the government took full control of everyone's lives. If you were conscripted then the military commanders told you what to do. But even farmers were told what to grow and how much and factories were told what to make and your food was rationed but then, when the war ended all of these support and command structures disappeared and you were on your own and it took quite a time to adjust. To match this sombre mood the electorate chose the austere Clement Attlee and the Labour party to replace the flamboyant wartime leader Winston Churchill in the July 1945 general election.

Churchill returned in 1951 at the start of 13 years of Tory rule. In 1955 Anthony Eden took over, then Harold Macmillan in 1957, then Lord Home in 1963. In 1964 Labour got their chance under Harold Wilson but in 1970 the Tories were back under Edward Heath.

There was one thing which the Fitzgeralds will have noticed in the early post war years which had not been seen by any of the previous occupants of our house; the sight of civilian aircraft landing and taking off from somewhere close by. Heathrow had been a small enthusiast's airfield since 1929 which was then taken over by the government in 1944 for military use but was never needed and was turned into a civil airport after the war, eventually becoming London Airport and replacing Croydon. The age of commercial air travel had begun. At first these regular sights may have been a novelty but in time they probably became a nuisance as aircraft were so much noisier in those days. One wonders whether George Cantopher, with his regular sea trips to Burma, and John Lehmann, and his to North America, would have taken the plane or continued to travel by ship.

By the 1960s things were beginning to brighten up and the "swinging sixties" started and Ealing had an important place in this. The Ealing Jazz club at 42A The Broadway, opposite Ealing Broadway station and barely a mile from our house opened its doors in January 1959. Early performers were Alexis Korner, Cyril Davies and Blues Incorporated. In 1962 Alexis Korner introduced Mick Jagger and Keith Richards to Brian Jones and the Rolling Stones first came together. Other regular musicians included Jack Bruce, Ginger Baker, Charlie Watts, Graham

Bond, Long John Baldry, Rod Stewart, Paul Jones, Manfred Mann, the Who and Eric Clapton. The club's contribution earned it a blue plaque.

In many ways the 1960s were similar to the 1930s. After the austerity and hardship of the previous decade there was a decade of reaction as confidence returned, sometimes, perhaps, going a little over the top.

One event during the 60s, which may have escaped the notice of a female household, occurred in 1966 when England won the World Cup just down the road in Wembley. The author's family were on holiday in the San Sebastian watching the matches on Spanish television with no great expectations. When England got to the final it was decided to return early to see the final at home and there was a mad scramble to make the ferry. Unfortunately the ferries were not sailing due to very rough seas and we had to watch the match in a café in Calais. We were shocked to find the French customers all supporting Germany and complete silence at the end.

Another feature of the 1960s, of interest perhaps to any remaining colonials or traders, was the progressive dismantlement of the Empire. Australia, New Zealand and Canada had been effectively self-governing for many years but following the war it was clear that independence would have to be granted to the others and this began with India and Pakistan in 1947. The 1960s saw independence granted to Barbados, Botswana, Cyprus, Guyana, Jamaica, Kenya, Malawi, Malta, Nigeria, Trinidad and Tobago and Zambia; the Union Jack was being lowered all over the world.

A further semi-constitutional change occurred in 1965. Following a Royal Commission on local government in Greater London, Middlesex ceased to exist and was swallowed up by London.

Virtually the entire history of our house so far has taken place in Middlesex. Ealing was, of course, in the County of Middlesex but so also was Paddington, where Thomas Richards was born as well as Hertford Street in Mayfair to which George Cantopher moved after our house. The dimensions of the county in 1965 are shown below; 1 and 2 are Potters Bar and Enfield, 5 is Tottenham, 25 and 26 are Twickenham and Sunbury. Ealing is 14. But in fact the County originally was even larger than this until in 1889 it lost about 20% of its area to the ever growing

County of London. The original boundaries of Middlesex had been the rivers Colne, Lee and Thames and a ridge of hills to the north. Incorporation into London was entirely logical but a pity for such an ancient Saxon territory (Middlesex is believed to be derived from the Middle Saxons). The only remaining relic of the original County is the Middlesex County Cricket team. John Betjeman was not highly amused by this change which in some ways resembles the way that Ealing took over from Brentford as described earlier.

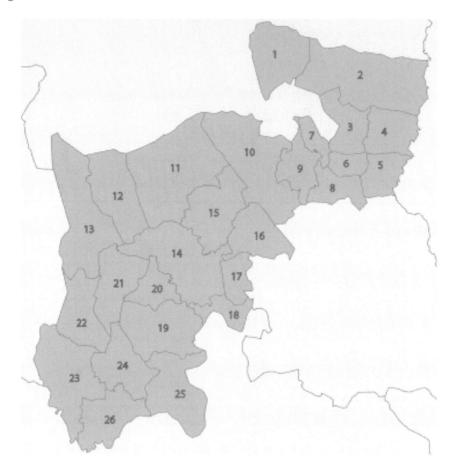

Another semi-constitutional change took place on 15th February 1971 when the United Kingdom decimalised its currency. Most readers who are younger than the writer will not remember that a pound used to be made up of 20 shillings and each shilling was made up of 12 pence. This made personal and even business accounting quite complicated. The first attempt to decimalise had been made in 1824 (following the introduction in 1795 of a decimal French Franc) but this was rejected by Parliament. It then took about 150 years before a simpler currency was introduced and the changeover went very smoothly. The value of the pound was unchanged but it now comprised 100 pennies and not 240 and we lost the "tanner" (6 pence or half a shilling) and the half-crown (2 shillings and 6 pence or one eighth of a pound)

And so, after 43 years in our house during which they had seen 5 monarchs (in the next 41 years the various residents to come would only know 1 monarch) endless Prime Ministers and governments, 2 counties, one Olympics (same for us) and one World War it was time for the Fitzgerald era to end and the 2 sisters sold our house in December 1972, barely a year after the death of their mother to John Leslie Harlow Kitchin and his wife, Maude Cecile Kitchin and the next chapter is theirs. But first, what were people wearing during this 30 year period?

The pictures below are not any of the Fitzgerald family but are simply to show how ordinary people dressed in the 1940s, 1950s and 1960s.

The 1940s

The 1950s

The swinging 1960s

And so now to the Kitchin family in 1972.

Chapter 18: The Kitchin Family 1973-77

John Leslie Harlow Kitchin was born 11th October 1924, the only son of Eric Kitchin and Muriel Harper. He was educated at Wolverhampton Grammar School and then at Worcester College, Oxford. It is likely that he did not complete his studies at Worcester College because in 1943 he enlisted with RAF Bomber Command. He would have been just 19 and could only have had one or two years at Oxford, and is not listed as an alumnus of Worcester College. Worcester College was founded in 1714 by the benefaction of Sir Thomas Cookes, a Worcestershire baronet, with the college gaining its name from the county of Worcestershire. Worcestershire is just down the road from Wolverhampton; is it fanciful to think this may have been the reason he chose this Oxford College?

The reason he did not complete his studies is because he was conscripted. Unlike other European countries, Britain had always relied on volunteers to fight in times of war. Conscription had been introduced in 1916 when more men were needed to fight in the trenches, but it was abandoned when the war ended. During the 1930s some men still chose to enter the armed forces after leaving school and in 1937 there were 200,000 soldiers in the British army. The government knew that this was not enough to fight a war with Germany and in April 1939 introduced the Military Training Act. The terms of the act meant that all men between the ages of 20 and 21 had to register for six months' military training. At the same time a list of 'reserved occupations' was published. This listed occupations that were essential to the war effort and stated that those employed in those jobs were exempt from conscription.

When war broke out in September 1939, some men volunteered to join the armed services, but Britain could still only raise 875,000 men. Other European countries had kept conscription between the wars and were able to raise much larger armies than Britain. In October 1939 the British government announced that all men aged between 18 and 41 who were not working in 'reserved occupations' could be called to join the armed services if required. The definition of reserved occupations changed during the war and was intended to cover workers who could not be spared at home, including medical practitioners, police officers and skilled workers in key industries such as coalmining and shipbuilding.

Conscription was by age and in October 1939 men aged between 20 and 23 were required to register to serve in one of the armed forces. They were allowed to choose between the army, the navy and the air force. As the war continued men from the other registered age groups received their 'call-up' papers requiring them to serve in the armed forces and this is what happened to John Kitchin and he chose RAF Bomber Command. He would have left Worcester College with a commitment that he could resume his studies when hostilities were over.

Bomber Command at that time was the most active of the 3 services. Service records are only available to family members and it is unknown what he did. If he was aircrew then he was certainly not shot down because details of evaders are publically available. He may well have been in one of the support services and in view of his later career perhaps his speciality was facilities management and building and runway architecture? It was fascinating to find that he had been in Bomber Command since the writer's father also served there and his remarkable escape story is told in full in *"Love is in the Air"* (available on Amazon) They were just 6 years different in age and one wonders if they ever met, perhaps at a post war RAF reception.

He completed his education after the war at the Birmingham School of Architecture between 1947, having then left the RAF, and 1952, where he earned his DipArch and eventual associate membership of the Royal Institute of British Architects. This must have been some sort of government or RAF retraining scheme because from 1947, having left the RAF, until 1961, he was on the electoral roll at 57 Charlwood Street in the Borough of Westminster, despite studying in Birmingham. This appears to have been some sort of government dormitory; there were lots of people there, indeed he may have continued living there following his marriage in 1956, he was certainly still registered there until 1961. Somehow also he must have retained his links with Oxford since in March 1950 the Western Morning News in Devon reported that "John Kitchin, captain of the Oxford golf team, inspired a victory over Cambridge in the 61st inter-Varsity golf match at Royal Lytham and St Anne's" It would be lovely to think that he was a member and played at Ealing golf club because we have featured this earlier but, sadly, the Club's records do not go back that far. .

Following his qualification he joined the Ministry of Education development group in 1952 as an assistant architect and he remained in the Ministry, in its various guises, for the rest of his working life.

He married Madeleine (often abbreviated to Maude) Cecile Coutant, daughter of Fernand and Renee of Reims, in 1956, and they had 2 sons and 1 daughter.

His career eventually took him to becoming the Chief Architect of the Department of Education and Science and in June 1981 the London Gazette recorded that he had been awarded a CB "to be an ordinary member of the Civil Division of the Third Class, or Companions, of the said most Honourable Order" essentially a knighthood (see later)

As a result of this award he will have attended Buckingham Palace and entered "Who's Who" during his lifetime and "Who was Who" after it, and that is where a lot of this detail came from. Sadly the award in June 1981 was just 6 months before he died on 24th January 1982, aged just 58. He had joined the Ministry of Education as an assistant architect in 1952 and during his career designed schools and buildings for handicapped children and youth and community projects. In 1965 he was head of the Building Productivity Group and he became Assistant Chief Architect in 1967 and Chief Architect in 1975. In this role he had a civil service rank of undersecretary, the 3rd highest rank after permanent secretary and deputy secretary. In his citation his recreation is noted as landscape painting.

The timing of his CB may well have been because the powers-that-be were aware of his condition and accelerated an award which might normally have been made on retirement. His address in 1982 was 5A Kensington Mansions, Trebovir Road, London SW5.

A CB is a Companion to the most Honourable Order of the Bath. As with so many decorations the history of this award dates back for centuries. The name derives from the elaborate mediaeval ceremony for creating a knight, which involved bathing (as a symbol of purification) as one of its elements. There are many different classes (GCB, KCB, DCB and so on) and CB would have been the normal award for a senior and respected civil servant, and made him Sir John Kitchin for his few remaining months.

The Kitchins bought our house in January 1973 when a charge, dated 22nd January, was registered in favour of South of England building society, Maidenhead. He was aged 49. It is quite possible that the house in 1973 was completely unchanged since it was first built and may even have been a bit of a wreck. It is almost certain that it was unchanged; prior to the Fitzgeralds the house was rented and landlords rarely make unnecessary changes, and anyway the house was still effectively new. Then there is the 45 years of occupation by the Fitzgeralds during most of which they were heavily indebted and probably could not afford to do much beyond maintaining the basic fabric. And then of course in the last 32 years the house was occupied by a widow and occasionally her children, together with her debts, and so it is quite likely that not only had no improvements been made but a degree of neglect may also have crept in.

What the house really needed now was an architect and that is what it got. John Kitchin made a large number of changes to our house and these are described below with the new layouts overlaying the originals.

The first thing was to install central heating throughout the house. Until now heating would have been either open fires or electric heaters but by the 1960s and early 1970s central heating became progressively more common. At the same time all the fireplaces except the one in the drawing room (still in use to this day) were sealed.

Then there was a loft conversion creating 2 extra bedrooms at the top of the house as well as a toilet. This necessitated a staircase up to the second floor which fitted neatly above the staircase on the plan from the ground floor to the first.

On the ground floor the wall separating the dining room and the drawing room was taken down to create one large lounge area, but still with the two door entrances. Of all the alterations this was the only loadbearing wall that required an RSJ.

The walls were removed that separated the morning room and vestibule making one large hallway In the kitchen area, the scullery, w.c. and coals room walls were all removed making one large kitchen and a w.c. was installed under the staircase opposite where the cycle house is shown and where the word "Hall" appears on the original design. All traces of the servant's area had gone.

Finally a doorway out onto the patio in the "L" shape between the Kitchen and Dining room was added (not shown below) and the side passage between our neighbour's house and ours was roofed over to create extra space and perhaps also for security reasons.

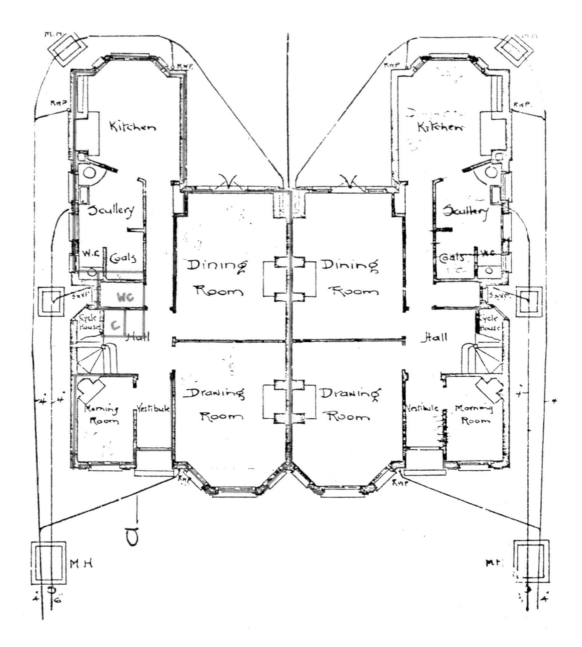

On the first floor (below) the smallest bedroom was dismantled thus enlarging the back bedroom and giving space for a shower/bath room, W.C. and a large cupboard (marked "C") to house the boiler necessitated by the newly installed central heating. Once again all trace of servant's quarters were gone. The large front bedroom is interesting. I had assumed that John Kitchin added the wall marked to create a dressing room. But if he had done this he would have gone to a lot of trouble since the door into the dressing room from the hallway is original and there is an original window in what is the party wall in the semidetached plans shown here. In fact the dressing room was built in the original house and this is the only difference between the Richards' houses in Lyncroft Gardens and those in Queens Walk/Gardens. Is it possible that Richards had intended Queens Walk and Queens Gardens to be semidetached as well (the Queens Walk plans are, as we have seen, based on those of Lyncroft) and then discovered that there was actually quite a slope in those roads, especially Queens Walk, that would have made building semis difficult and that is the reason they are detached thus explaining the window? Or were the north Ealing versions planned for a more gentrified clientele that would require a changing room?

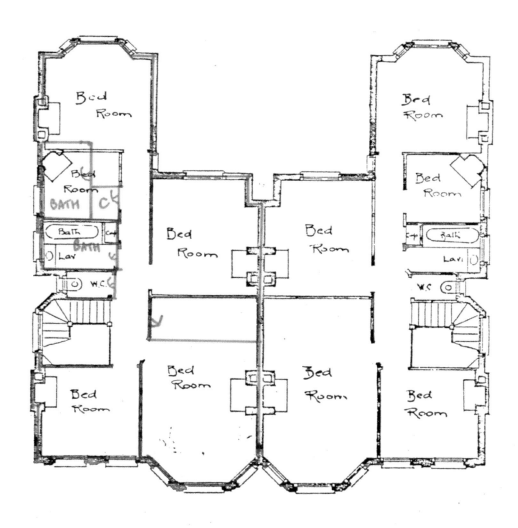

E   *8 FEET TO ONE INCH.*

This all amounts to a huge amount of work and must have taken the best part of a year to complete and one would normally wish to stay in a property for a long time to reap the rewards of the considerable cost and effort. But the Kitchins moved out in 1977 having lived in the house just 4 years. Perhaps John Kitchin's continued career advancement meant he needed to be nearer the office. It is also difficult to understand why he had the loft conversion done creating a 6 bedroom house when they only had 3 children.

The picture below will be remembered by anyone who watched the Frost Report in 1966 and its skit on the class war. The bowler hatted man is John Cleese but is also dressed exactly as a civil servant of the 1960s would have dressed and may bear a passing resemblance to John Kitchin.

Constitutionally Edward Heath was Prime Minister 1970 – 74 and took this country into the Common Market in 1973 (having been rejected by General de Gaulle's "Non" 10 years earlier). Harold Wilson was then a Prime Minister for the second time from 1974-76 and allowed a referendum on Common Market membership in 1975 which, remarkably, voted 67% in favour. James Callaghan followed Wilson from 1976-79.

Musically, if the swinging sixties were the decade of the Beatles and the Rolling Stones, then the 70s were the decade of hard rock; Alice Cooper, Deep Purple, Led Zeppelin, AC/DC, and Black Sabbath amongst many others. But there was also glam rock and the ultimate exponents of this were the group called Queen. Their singer, perhaps leader, was Freddie Mercury and he has links with this story. His parents were Parsis from Bombay who moved to Zanzibar so his father could continue his job as a cashier at the British Colonial Office (which post Indian independence had ceased to exist in India) Freddie was born in Zanzibar in 1946 but spent a lot of his childhood in India. By 1964 there was widespread persecution of Arabs and Indians in Zanzibar and the family fled, coming to live in Feltham, Middlesex (but, as we have seen, it would only be Middlesex for one year after they arrived) Freddie studied art at Ealing Art College (now the University of West London) and, with his remarkable 4 octave range, he wrote many of Queen's greatest hits, including Bohemian Rhapsody. He died in 1991.

And so we now move on to our penultimate residents, the Oakleys.

Chapter 19: The Oakley Family 1977-82

Now in its 76th year our house welcomed the Oakleys, its 6th owners (following Thomas Richards, Frank Handover, William Burnham, Edward Fitzgerald and family and John Kitchin) and 7th occupants (following Albert Boehr, John Richmond, George Cantopher, John Lehmann, Edward Fitzgerald and family and John Kitchin) Over 76 years this is quite a small turnover but this is of course distorted by the Fitzgerald tenure of 45 years; apart from them no one else stayed longer than the average London tenure of about 5 to 10 years, and the Oakleys were no exception to this although their successors, the writer and his family, have been.

In 1977 Robin and Ann Oakley bought the house and moved in. They will have had the benefit of a newly renovated house courtesy of John Kitchin. The house would now be occupied by a pair of young academics. Just as the social and political history of the times, or some of it, has emerged from the occupants of the house, one of the next owners, Ann Oakley, brings two very important 20th century developments to the story, one directly, through her own work, on feminism and gender in relation to domestic life, health, social science and public policy, and the other, indirectly, through her father, who died 4 years before she moved in, the welfare state. Ann Oakley is the house's most nationally prominent resident, even more distinguished, in a different way, than her knighted predecessor.

Ann Oakley's father was Richard Titmuss who is regarded as one of the founding fathers of Britain's welfare state.

Richard Morris Titmuss (1907 – 1973) was a pioneering policy analyst and teacher. He founded the academic discipline of Social Administration (now largely known in universities as Social Policy) and held the founding chair in the subject at the London School of Economics and, in his honour, the Richard Titmuss Chair in Social Policy was created. He held his chair from 1950, after brief spells in the Cabinet Office and the Social Medicine Research Unit, until his death in 1973.

His books and articles in the 1950s helped to define the characteristics of Britain's post WWII welfare state and of a universal welfare society, in ways that parallel the contributions of Gunnar Myrdal in Sweden and he has often been called one of the pioneers of the Welfare State. He also contributed to a number of government committees on the health service and social policy.

His concerns focused especially on issues of social justice. His final and perhaps most important book, *The Gift Relationship,* expressed his own philosophy of altruism in social and health policy and, like much of his work, emphasized his preference for the values of public service over private or commercial forms of care.

Today we take the Welfare State for granted but before the Second World War most welfare was run by private volunteer organisations and parishes and provision was patchy at best. It was only in 1930 that workhouses were finally abolished although many continued as "Public Assistance" institutions until even these were abolished in 1948 and the last vestiges of the Poor Laws disappeared. Churchill had commissioned William Beveridge to write a report on what should replace these arrangements after the war and Beveridge identified the 5 "giants on the road to post war reconstruction" as being poverty, disease, ignorance, squalor and idleness" and his famous report dealt with all of these, and Richard Titmuss played an important part in this. With all the best intentions the idea that the State must do everything had arrived.

Richard Titmuss' post war home until he died was 32 Twyford Avenue, Acton, barely 2 miles from our house and his academic contributions were acknowledged by an English Heritage blue plaque as shown below.

When the blue plaque was unveiled in October 2011, Ann said 'My father's work established social administration as a scientific discipline, and pioneered an analysis of social policy based on both science and ethics. His defence of the 'good society' was egalitarian, rationalist and mindful of human beings' need for a sense of social connection. What he had to say is hugely relevant to the social problems we face today, and particularly to the escalating divisions of a class society which has lost its way in prioritising welfare as the right of all citizens.' Richard Titmuss was appointed CBE in 1966. Yours truly studied sociology at Southampton University and heard much about Richard Titmuss little expecting that I would eventually buy his daughter's house.

Ann Titmuss had married Robin Oakley in 1964, aged 20. She has been as distinguished and productive as her father. The following is extracted from the extensive coverage of her work that is publically available. She is described as "a distinguished sociologist, feminist, and writer".

She was educated at Somerville College, Oxford University taking her BA in 1965 (Politics, Philosophy and Economics) Somerville College was founded in 1879 as one of the first women's colleges in Oxford (male students were admitted from 1994) The list of her fellow alumni, not necessarily contemporaneous, is remarkable; A.S.Byatt, Marghanita Laski, Dilys Powell, Margaret Thatcher, Indira Ghandi, Iris Murdoch, Dorothy Sayers and Shirley Williams amongst many others.

In the next few years after university she wrote scripts for children's television and wrote numerous short stories and had two novels rejected by publishers. Returning to formal education at Bedford College, University of London, she gained a PhD in 1974; the qualification

116

was a study of housework as work and 2 books came out of it "The Sociology of Housework" and "Housework" both published in the same year.

Much of her sociological research focused on medical sociology and women's health. She has also made important contributions to debates about sociological research methods.

Ann Oakley has written numerous academic works, many focusing on the lives and roles of women in society as well as several best-selling novels, of which the best-known is probably *The Men's Room*, which was adapted by Laura Lamson for BBC television in 1991, and which starred Harriet Walter and Bill Nighy. She has also written an early partial autobiography. She divides her life between living in London and in a rural house where she does most of her fiction writing. She is a mother and grandmother.

For the first 27 years of our house women did not have the vote. Neither Mrs Boehr, nor Mrs Richmond, Mrs Cantopher nor Mrs Lehmann participated in elections, Mrs Fitzgerald was the first. The house also waited 78 years before it saw the first British female Prime Minister (only the 5th female head of state in the world after Sirimavo Bandaranaike in Sri Lanka, Indira Ghandi in India, Golda Meir in Israel and Elisabeth Domitien in the Central African Republic) There was much for Ann Oakley to write about.

She is Professor of Sociology and Social Policy at the Institute of Education, University of London, and until January 2005 was Director of the Social Science Research Unit (SSRU) at the Institute, where she also headed the Evidence for Policy and Practice Information and Coordinating (EPPI-Centre). She holds honorary appointments as a Professor in Social Sciences at the Institute of Child Health in London (now lapsed) and as a Fellow at Somerville College in Oxford. In 2011 the British Sociological Association gave her one of their first Lifetime Achievement Awards for her extraordinary contribution to the history of the development of sociology in Britain. She now works on research part-time, and spends the rest of it writing, wondering what to do about her archives, developing environmentally friendly cleaning products, and looking after her grandchildren.

To show the scale of her prodigious output a selection is shown below.

Non Fiction

- (1972) *Sex, Gender and Society*. London: Temple Smith. Reprinted with new Introduction, London: Gower, 1985.
- (1974) *Housewife*. London: Allen Lane.
- (1974) *The Sociology of Housework*. London: Martin Robertson. Reprinted with new Introduction. Oxford: Basil Blackwell, 1985 (also translated into German, Dutch and Japanese).
- (1976) *Woman's Work: The Housewife, Past and Present*. New York: Random House. (Re-titled version of *Housewife* – 1974)
- (1979) *Becoming a Mother*. Oxford: Martin Robertson. (Under the title *From Here to Maternity*. Harmondsworth: Penguin, 1981. Reprinted with new Introduction, 1986.)

- (1980) *Women Confined: Towards a sociology of childbirth*. Oxford: Martin Robertson.
- (1981) *Subject Women*. Oxford: Martin Robertson.
- (1984) *The Captured Womb: A history of the medical care of pregnant women*. Oxford: Basil Blackwell.
- (1984) *Taking it Like a Woman*. London: Jonathan Cape. (Paperback published Fontana 1985; also published by Random House, New York).
- (1986) *Telling the Truth about Jerusalem: Selected essays*. Oxford: Basil Blackwell.
- (1986) *The rights and Wrongs of women* (Selected essays edited with Juliet Mitchell).
- (1986) *What is Feminism?* (Selected essays edited with Juliet Mitchell).
- (1992) *Social Support and Motherhood: The natural history of a research project*. Oxford: Basil Blackwell.
- (1993) *Essays on Women, Medicine and Health*. Edinburgh: Edinburgh University Press.
- (1996) *Man and Wife: Richard and Kay Titmuss, my parents' early years*. London: HarperCollins.
- (1997) *Who's Afraid of Feminism?* London: Hamish Hamilton. (New York: The New Press.) (edited with Juliet Mitchell).
- (1997) *The Gift Relationship: From human blood to social policy*. By Richard M Titmuss. London: LSE Books. (New York: The New Press.) (edited with John Ashton).
- (2000) *Experiments in Knowing: Gender and method in the social sciences*. Cambridge: Polity Press. (New York: The New Press.)
- (2001) *Welfare & Wellbeing: Richard Titmuss's contribution to Social Policy*, (edited with Peter Alcock, Howard Glennerster & Adrian Sinfield), Bristol: Policy Press.
- (2002) *Gender on Planet Earth*. Cambridge: Polity Press (New York: The New Press, 2003).
- (2004) *Private Complaints & Public Health: Richard Titmuss on the National Health Service*, (edited, with Jonathan Barker), Bristol: Policy Press.
- (2007) *Fracture: Adventures of a broken body*, Bristol: Policy Press.

Fiction

- (1989) *The Men's Room*. London: Virago. (HarperCollins paperback 1989; New York: Atheneum, 1989.) (televised)
- (1990) (under the nom de plume Rosamund Clay) *Only Angels Forget*. London: Virago.
- (1991) *Matilda's Mistake*. London: Virago (HarperCollins paperback, 1991).
- (1992) *The Secret Lives of Eleanor Jenkinson*. London: HarperCollins.
- (1993) *Scenes Originating in the Garden of Eden*. London: HarperCollins.
- (1995) *Where the bee sucks*, in: (eds) Jones RG, Williams AS. *The Penguin Book of Erotic Stories by Women*. London: Penguin Books, pp. 384–397.
- (1995) *Death in the egg*, in: (eds) Williams AS, Jones RG. *The Penguin Book of Modern Fantasy by Women*. London: Penguin Books, pp. 525–532.
- (1996) *A Proper Holiday*. London: HarperCollins.
- (1999) *Overheads*. London: HarperCollins.

Ann Oakley's picture, below, is taken from her web site. In her 'spare' time Ann admits to enjoying swimming, classical ballet, rural life, music and the company of her family and friends, especially her grandchildren.

Robin Oakley was born in 1940 in Hildenborough in the Weald of Kent and went to Cambridge in 1959 to study social sciences and followed this with a post-graduate Diploma in Social Anthropology and a D.Phil in Sociology at Oxford. From the mid-1960s until the early 1980s he was on the Sociology faculty of the University of London.

For more than forty years he has also been an independent consultant specialising in assisting public authorities and NGOs in addressing issues of racism and ethnic relations, and he has written widely on these subjects. He is an Honorary Research Fellow at the Centre for Minority Studies, Royal Holloway, University of London, and a Runnymede Fellow at The Runnymede Trust.

In Britain, he has undertaken research, training and consultancy for a wide range of professional groups and public bodies, especially in the fields of policing and criminal justice, central and local government, and education. He has also worked extensively on these issues with voluntary and community associations, especially at the local level.

At a European level he has worked on a variety of projects on discrimination and minority issues (especially relating to Roma), both with Inter-Governmental and other European organisations and in individual countries across both Western and Central/Eastern Europe, and he has regularly acted as a consultant for the Council of Europe.

His recent activities include working on policing and minority/Roma issues with the OSCE High Commissioner on National Minorities and the ODIHR, on tackling racist violence and related issues with the EU Monitoring Centre on Racism (now EU Fundamental Rights Agency), on the integration of Roma at the local level with the NGO European Dialogue and the CoE Congress of Local & Regional Authorities, and in the UK, on preventing racist violence among young people with The Runnymede Trust & The Trust for London.

Robin has been no less productive than Ann and his principal European-level publications and reports include:

Police Training Concerning Migrants & Ethnic Relations, CoE 1994

Tackling Racist & Xenophobic Violence in Europe: Review & Practical Guidance, CoE 1996

Tackling Racist & Xenophobic Violence in Europe: Case-Studies, CoE 1997

Practical Examples in Combating Racism against Roma/Gypsies, CoE/ECRI 2001

Promoting Roma Integration at Local Level: Guidance for NGOs & Public Authorities, European Dialogue 2005

Policing Racist Crime and Violence: A Comparative Analysis, EUMC (now EU FRA) 2005

(as Consultant) Recommendations on Policing in Multi-Ethnic Societies, OSCE/HCNM 2006

Policing and Minorities in the Russian Federation: Key International Documents and Case Studies, CoE 2008

The Situation of Roma in Europe: A Challenge for Local & Regional Authorities, CoE/CLRA 2011

Robin is pictured below.

The period of the Oakley's occupation was a very difficult one nationally. James Callaghan was Prime Minister from April 1976 to May 1979 having succeeded Harold Wilson. This was a period of severe difficulty with the Trades Unions. Both inflation and unemployment were very high,

the government had to negotiate IMF loans to be able to sustain the country and this all culminated in the "winter of discontent" of 1978/9 when there were widespread strikes, including by gravediggers and refuse collectors, power shortages and an imposed 3 day working week and all this coincided with an exceptionally cold winter and it was generally a thoroughly miserable time. It was an economic dark age in which the country had been brought to its knees and was widely described as "the sick man of Europe" Richard Titmuss' values of public service and altruism were in very short supply. It was resolved by the general election of May 1979 when an alumnus of Somerville College, Oxford, by the name of Margaret Thatcher was elected Prime Minister with a 43 seat majority. A famous piece of political advertising used in 1979 is shown below with a dole queue snaking towards a benefits office. The advert was designed by Saatchi and Saatchi and has been widely used all over the world including recently in the USA "Obama isn't working". It would be 18 years before the electorate would trust Labour with government again, 13 years with Margaret Thatcher and 5 with John Major, and they would have to rebrand themselves as "New Labour" to distance themselves from the disastrous Wilson and Callaghan years.

The next couple of years were spent legislating controls over union power that would prevent a repetition of the past few years. Soon after this was achieved another challenge faced the government; in April 1982 Argentina invaded the Falklands and it took until the 14th June before the Islands were freed. In 1962 Dean Achieson, Secretary of State under Truman had said "Britain has lost an Empire and has yet to find a role in the world" After all the retrenchment and dismantlement of the Empire in the 1950s and 60s the Falklands finally gave the country a success and with an economy that was now recovering strongly this was undoubtedly a major national turning point from a very low level.

Shortly before the Oakleys moved out in 1982, the Gleesons (Tim and Eileen and daughters Paula and Carla) moved in next door and thus predate us by a few months, and are, so far as I know, the longest residents in the road.

And now it is time to turn to the writer and his family.

Chapter 20: The Pack Family 1982 – present

Well, this is us and we arrived in 1982. The family picture below was taken in the last few years and is more or less how we look now.

The picture below was taken shortly after we moved into the house and includes the writer's parents, brother and sister in law and nephews. We are the foursome clustered around and behind my father on the left side of the picture.

Our arrival had 2 small hiccups. We were looking for a larger house and Jacky had phoned me at work to go and see a property straight from work. I presented myself at 5 Queens Walk only to be told it was not for sale and perhaps I was thinking of 5 Queens Gardens, just round the corner. I comfort myself that the postman and newspaper boy regularly make the same mistake.

The second hiccup came when the solicitors were doing their conveyancing work and came across a covenant dated 16th November 1865 by a certain Henry de Bruno Austin, who we have encountered earlier; they quickly realised it was not an issue. Henry de Bruno Austin certainly made his mark – every time the house was bought and sold his name will have come up, and almost certainly for many other properties as well.

And so after a German refugee junior clerical worker (Albert Boehr) a carpenter (John Richmond) a rice merchant (George Cantopher) a condensed milk and starch merchant (John Lehmann) a GPO civil servant (Edward Fitzgerald) a Department of Education architect (John Kitchin) and a writer and academic (Ann Oakley) we moved in.

Since this is a history of the house I will make our family biography brief. The writer was born in 1946 in London and Jacky was born at a later date in Rugby, Warwickshire. We married in 1970 having met at Southampton University. Some while later Arabella and Joe joined us. We have lived most of our married life in London, and 31 of our 43 married years in this house. 5 of our married years were spent in Geneva, where the writer's job at the time took him, and it was on returning to London that we bought this house. The writer's career was in finance and Jacky's was in higher education at Thames Valley University. Arabella is a qualified accountant and Joe specialises in direct marketing.

In the 31 years we have lived in our house the immediate area has changed remarkably little. The built environment has hardly changed at all. There have been some small infill developments (including behind our house where a small cluster of new houses has taken over what was a children's playground area for the nearby flats) and wherever you see new(ish) houses in the middle of Victorian or Edwardian houses that is where WW2 bombs have fallen. In essence our area and much of residential Ealing was substantially built by the end of the 1st World War. A time traveller from 50 years ago would have little trouble finding their way around. A time traveller from 100 years ago would however notice 3 big changes, but not to the houses.

Trees

Charles Jones, the Borough Surveyor during much of the development of Ealing and our area in particular was very keen on street trees and is the reason Ealing is known as a leafy suburb. Many of the roads in Ealing bear testament to this and Ealing remains a very leafy suburb but now some of the 100+ year old trees are becoming very large as the picture below of our road shows. Most of the originally planted and very large trees are London plane and Lime, in recent years other varieties have been used; they would have been a tenth the size when planted.

Cars

This is of course not unique to this area. The first 4 residents of the house will have known only horses and carts with perhaps the very occasional motorised vehicle. The Fitzgeralds will have been the first to see more than just a handful of vehicles, especially post war, and it will be from the Kitchins onwards that, like many suburban areas, 2, 3 and even 4 car families have become the norm. Of the 9 Thomas Richards houses in our road we are 1 of only 3 that haven't (yet) converted our front garden to a parking lot. As Controlled Parking Zones encroach on all sides, and parking for the local shops, schools and stations increases it becomes harder to resist this trend.

Pitshanger Lane

 The evolution of Pitshanger Lane will have been a big surprise to the time traveller from 100 years ago; in fact he would have been amazed. In 1901 Pitshanger Lane was still a farm track that led only to the fields around. It was surfaced around 1906 to allow the building of the Brentham estate and then was gradually developed itself with houses, and it was in this year that the first shop appeared, the Coop at the north western end of the Lane. North Ealing was developing quickly and residents needed shops with Ealing Broadway too far away and so the houses on Pitshanger Lane gradually got converted to shops. Today the Lane is as shown below (the Cooperative store visible on the right of the picture is not on the site of the original store, that was opposite and behind the camera).

A roll call of the establishments along the Lane sums up the area extremely well. There are 3 female hairdressers and 2 male, 5 cafes, 10 restaurants/takeaways (2 French, 2 Pizzas, a Chinese, Greek, Japanese, Indian, Kebab and Fish and chips) plus a pub/restaurant (named inevitably "The Village Inn") 4 Dry Cleaners, 3 estate agents, 2 pharmacies, 2 flower shops, 2 Coops, 2 Charity Shops, 2 Gift shops, 2 general stores and an Interior design shop, an off license, a Dance studio, a children's clothes shop, a pet shop, a betting shop, a newsagent, a delicatessen, a dentist, an osteopath, a funeral parlour, a Maths and English Tuition centre, a baker, a heel bar, a furniture store, a beautician, a butcher, a fruit and vegetable shop, a wet fishmonger, a bookshop, a library, a manicure and massage parlour and an optician. In addition to these there are also St Barnabas Anglican church, a Methodist church and North Ealing primary school. This is all that the prosperous and middle class residents could want and just over 100 years ago it was a farm track.

There is a very active organisation called the Pitshanger Community Association that organises 2 local events every year; "Party in the Park", held in June in Pitshanger park, and "Light up the Lane" at the start of the Christmas season. They also represent residents on local issues such as CPZ proposals made by the Council and promote the image of the area as Pitshanger Village. They were also very active, on behalf of residents and shopowners when Tesco tried to acquire the property that is now a Maths and English Tuition centre.

Our neighbours over the years have demonstrated perfectly the history of this part of north Ealing. When we moved in the neighbours to one side were the Nickersons; Basil was the deputy head at St Benedict's School and Claire was the school secretary. To the other side Tim was a set designer for the BBC ("Only fools and horses" "Porridge" "The 2 Ronnies" and many more) and Eileen was an English teacher at St Benedict's. Further down the road was Mavis Davis who worked at the BBC. There is also Philip, a cameraman, and Barbara, an artist. In number one a Polish family have lived for many years (although arriving after us) In an earlier chapter we saw that William Burnham bought numbers 5 and 9 Queens Gardens in 1910 and occupied the latter himself and rented out the former. Number 9 is now owned by an estate agent which seems appropriate.

Bob and Sue Jones lived at number 15 for 31 years until 2007, the same as our occupation to date. Their children are Duncan and Catherine and Duncan ("Dunc the hunk") used to babysit our children. They bought the property from an extended family who had owned it through generations since it was built shortly after ours in 1902, an astonishing 74 years, although between 1948 and 1976 it was rented out. Number 15 has thus only had three ownerships over its entire life.

The Joneses report that "in the 1920s and 30s a member of the original owning family was a keen radio ham, and we found lots of postcards from his fellow hams around the world in the loft when we moved in. There was also still in place a very tall radio mast (a kind of wooden telegraph pole thing) at the bottom of the garden. This was secured by four wire ropes tethered to large blocks of concrete set into the garden. They took a great deal of removing!" And a further recollection "when we moved in we remember Mrs Cove and her mother lived just a few houses down and the old lady reminisced about walking to Hanger Lane through green fields, which started just beyond No. 17" (the end of the Richards houses).

The writer is a member of Ealing golf club and has been for almost as long as we have lived here. My parents used to live in Fowlers Walk on the Brentham estate. We go to concerts at St Marys and St Barnabas, and to Parish lunches at St Benedicts. We saw earlier that George Cantopher, who lived in our house from 1910 to 1917 named the property "Rockcliffe" We will make the convenient assumption that he decided to do this in 1913 and thus that our reinstatement of the name (pictured below) marks the centenary of the original naming.

The sign is not on the front door, to do that you have to apply to the Post Office and we did not wish to make the postman's job harder. Instead it is on the back door, the tradesman's entrance as was, in its time the busiest entrance to the house.

The Occupants

The theme of this book has been to trace the history of the house through its occupants. Inevitably details of the occupants have varied between sketchy and almost non-existent. But this does not stop one forming a view of them, no matter how inaccurate this may be. Human beings are naturally judgemental even if often wrong. And when thinking of previous residents one wonders which rooms they liked to sit in, whether they enjoyed the garden and what it was like then and so on. So here goes, on the basis of insufficient information, my character assessment of the principal characters.

Thomas Richards (owner 1901-06)

There has already been a degree of character assassination for Thomas Richards in the earlier chapter. There do seem to be good grounds to believe that it was his wife, Madge, who pushed him along, who lifted him from articled clerk to owning his own law firm and then going into property speculation (with some disastrous results) and then made him (them) a very wealthy couple (was this a start of the feminism that would conclude with Ann Oakley?) They do not appear to have had time for a family and he does not appear to have had any other interests and when she died he lost his driving force and did not know what to do or who to leave his wealth to other than to the 3 partners in his firm who were almost certainly very rich people anyway and did not need it. It seems like a sad, rather driven and obsessional life although one must acknowledge that as the son of a Butler and Lace cleaner from a small Paddington house he had nonetheless done extraordinarily well.

Albert Boehr (occupier 1901-06)

In his chapter we concluded that Albert Boehr was a modestly prosperous white collar worker with a large and occasionally difficult family that may have been expensive to support. They moved all over south London renting properties as their fortunes and their family waxed and waned, never prosperous enough to buy a property. He was 55 when they came to our house and they still had 3 or 4 children at home. They must have been absolutely delighted to come to Queens Gardens and live in a villa, perhaps with more space than they had ever known, even if it was surrounded for a few years by a building site, which will probably not have bothered them at all. They will have almost certainly have known that their tenancy would be short lived and would end at Thomas Richards' whim when the property became saleable but their rental was probably nominal and they were quite used to moving around. Albert Boehr must have been a decent and honourable man or Thomas Richards would not have entrusted one of his houses to him and, for no particularly good reason, one feels well-disposed towards him.

Frank Handover (owner 1906-10)

He bought the property in 1906, aged just 24 and an architect's assistant. He must have been helped in the purchase by his father-in-law-to-be James Holloway, a "boarding house keeper"

Whilst in today's terms this sounds a highly suspicious profession it probably means less than a hotel but more than a B+B. Having bought the property Frank and his new wife never moved in and sold it 4 years later. During these 4 years the area was still very busy with building and it is possible that Frank's wife simply did not like the house that had been bought unbeknownst to her or perhaps she was never going to like a house that she hadn't chosen? Frank comes over, again for no particular reason, as a bit of a kept man. He was living with the Holloways before he was married, was persuaded by father-in-law to buy a house which his wife then did not like, and which was then sold at a loss. Prior to the sale the house was rented to John Richmond.

John Richmond (occupier 1906-10)

There is little enough to go on with the others but for John Richmond there is almost nothing and certainly not enough for a character assessment. He was almost certainly a carpenter/labourer probably installed for the same reasons as Albert Boehr, to house-sit until the property became saleable. It may be that he was able to afford a reduced rent because he was working on the building of the Brentham estate

William Burnham (owner 1910-27)

William Burnham bought the house in 1910 at the same time as buying number 9 where he lived. In 1910 he was aged 60 and had been retired 10 years and so had obviously been successful as a bank cashier. Having lived mainly in St John's Wood and Hampstead before Ealing this was presumably his country retirement and number 5 was his pension. He must have been quite shrewd; he acquired our house, only 9 years after it was built, for 22% less than it cost Thomas Richards to build it. William Burnham rented the house for 17 years to the 2 tenants who follow.

George Cantopher (occupier 1910-17)

George Cantopher was a highly exotic colonial who was a merchant in the Burma Rice trade and is a species rarely encountered these days. He was almost certainly the precise market that Thomas Richards had targeted 9 years earlier. He became a wealthy man and lived in Mayfair after our house and before retiring to the Isle of Wight and one assumes that you didn't become wealthy in the Rice Trade ("The Devil's Business" or "The Grand National of Commerce") by being a shrinking violet.

John Lehmann (occupier 1917-27)

John Lehmann was the 11th of 11 children in a family of Swiss immigrants. His professional life was condensed milk and starch. He clearly made a lot of money but appears to have had no airs and graces; after our house he moved to a slightly larger one in Mattock Lane rather than a Mayfair address as his predecessor had done. Perhaps it is an instinctive liking for the Swiss French (having lived there 5 years) or perhaps condensed milk and starch is such a quirky thing to specialise in or perhaps it is because John Lehmann appears to have been a family man moving back to Mattock Lane for the rest of his life; for all these reasons I think instinctively he was a good guy.

Edward and Amelia Fitzgerald (owner/occupiers 1927-73)

Edward was a son of an iterant Irish family and somehow he ran up some serious debts. He died aged 63 in 1940 and left Amelia with some big problems, not excluding a world war in progress. It would be not until 1963 when she was 83 years old that the debts were finally extinguished. Did they simply overextend themselves in buying the property, or was it a problem of gambling or other vices, or perhaps school fees for their daughters or medical bills, or unwise investments, or perhaps a combination of all of these? There is no information to give any guidance and perhaps one doesn't want any. All one can hope is that despite all the difficulties they were happy. To have stayed so long they must have liked the house otherwise surely they would have sold it as quickly as possible to get rid of the debts.

John Kitchin (owner/occupiers 1973-77)

One feels warmly towards the Kitchins. He was an RAF officer in Bomber Command, as was my father and RAF types are invariably trustworthy, loyal and level headed. He chose a French wife which is admirable and, of course, he made the changes to the house from which all subsequent owners have benefited.

Ann and Robin Oakley (1977-82)

Ann and Robin Oakley are the only previous residents still living, although some of the earlier ones may well have descendants that I have not traced, and so I will not offer any character comments at all.

Jeff and Jacky Pack (1982 – present)

One cannot offer character observations about ourselves. Only the House itself will know if my character observations above have any accuracy. The house has seen a surprising variety of occupants. The first two were working class families (for particular reasons) then a classic colonial trader (in today's terms perhaps a super-rich and obnoxious banker) then another trader, but this one was gentler and more normally middle class, then a struggling Irish family, then a middle class civil servant, then academics and then us. One strange thing is that until the Kitchins almost all the occupiers (except perhaps John Richmond) were of foreign descent – Boehr from Poland/Germany, Cantopher born in Bengal, Lehmann in Switzerland, Fitzgerald was a son of an Irish family, and even John Kitchin had a French wife. Ealing is often referred to as being highly multicultural and it is clear that it always has been.

Endnote

When starting this book I half expected it to have tinges of a ghost story about it. One inevitably wonders about the people who lived here before us; which rooms did they sit in, were they loud, what they did to the garden, were they happy and what were their stories. I can't claim to have properly answered many, if any, of these questions but hope that the House is happy to have part of its story told.

In writing the book the House seems to have developed a personality of its own, it predates us and will postdate us as well; whilst we are the nominal owners, or guardians, for the present others will follow and one wonders who will occupy it for the next 112 years. To date there have been artisans, professionals and academics but so far no creative occupants in the artistic sense; perhaps the House might yearn for some musicians in years to come? But the main thing one hopes for is that future occupants should be families and the house should not suffer the indignity of being turned into flats. The Fitzgeralds occupied the house for 45 years, we are in our 31st year, will we overtake them before the music arrives?

There is a wealth of old pictures of Ealing at the public library and the final pages will be taken up with a selection of what the area was like before Charles Jones, Thomas Richards, Henry Vivian and many others changed it forever. These scenes may appear to be of a forgotten and long ago world, but it is not so long ago, my grandfather (himself a builder) was 16 when our house was built and had he journeyed by horse and trap from Kent to Ealing at round about that time then these would have been the scenes to greet him. Just before the house was built north Ealing was a delightful mixture of grand villas, Castlebar villas in 1880 are shown below.

But no more than hundreds of yards away from the villas is open countryside as shown in the next 4 pictures.

This picture and all the ones that follow are courtesy of Ealing library

Argyle Road in 1890

Argyle Road in 1902

By The Same Author

Love Is In The Air: *The wartime letters & memories of Joe Pack and Margaret Dillon*

Woodfield 2008 | ISBN 1-84683-046-X | 280 pages | softback | 140 x 205 mm | £9.95

This book is compiled from two main sources ~ the wartime memoir of Joe Pack, an RAF pilot and the many letters he exchanged with his wife-to-be whilst serving overseas during World War 2.

Joe saw plenty of action, both in the air and on the ground, firstly in Europe and later in Africa and the Indian Ocean. Born in 1918 and raised in the village of Egerton in rural Kent, Joe volunteered for the RAF in 1940 and was rapidly trained as a pilot. Just over a year later he was posted to an operational heavy bomber squadron (No.35) based at Linton-on-Ouse in Yorkshire. He flew a Halifax bomber on operations over enemy territory between January and June 1942 until the night of 7/8 June when, on his 18th 'Op', his aircraft was shot down over the Dutch/German border.

His evasion and return to the UK involved the famous Comète line ~ plus the efforts of a Dutch Inspector of ditches, a Basque smuggler and many other extraordinary people who put their own lives at risk to help stranded allied airmen evade capture.

On his return he was reassigned to flying boats ~ first Sunderlands and then Catalinas ~ and while undergoing the extra training this required, his eye was caught by a certain Margaret Dillon, a WAAF Officer serving at RAF Oban. His amorous advances were rejected, however, and she was subsequently posted to RAF Davidstow Moor in Cornwall, whilst he was destined to join 265 Squadron on patrol in the Indian Ocean.

Romance seemed well-and-truly off the menu, but at some point ~ and it is not clear exactly when or why ~ they began corresponding. The many airmail letters they subsequently exchanged, charmingly document their developing courtship and reveal many fascinating details about the wartime lives of two young people separated by extraordinary events.

~~~

A Cornucopia of Packs: *An informal history of the Pack family*

Woodfield 2010 | ISBN 1-84683-104-0 | softback | 205 x 290 mm | 240 pages | £15 (b/w version) / £25 (full colour version)

In this enjoyable family history, Jeffrey Pack takes a look at the activities of the Pack family over several centuries and demonstrates how addictive genealogy can be.

The author succeeded in tracing his own forebears back about 250 years but, in the course of his research, he also discovered many additional bearers of the Pack surname who were quite possibly related to his own branch of the family but with whom he could not definitively establish a link.

This wider history of the Pack family name goes back 500 years and includes such luminaries as Sir Christopher Pack, Lord Mayor of London in 1654 and a close friend of Oliver Cromwell; Sir Denis Pack, second (after Wellington) most decorated hero of Waterloo; Thomas Pack, who ran the Whitechapel Bell Foundry, the most famous in the world; Packs who emigrated to the USA and elsewhere; Packs who ended up in the workhouse; a possible Mormon Pack; a Barnardo's Pack ... and much more besides. The author sets the stories of these colourful individuals in context within the wider history of the times in which they lived and, in some cases, played significant roles.

He also examines the history of Egerton – the village in Kent where the Pack surname proliferated and which has been home to many generations of Packs over the centuries.

The outcome is an entertaining and informative journey through several hundred years of English social history that will prove fascinating to present-day members of the Pack family in particular, but also makes for agreeable reading in its own right.

~~~

The Enigma of 13 Sandown Road

Woodfield 2012 | ISBN 1-84683-137-7 | softback | 230 pages | £9.95

An elderly man dies in his modest south London house. There is nothing apparently suspicious about his death. His house is eventually bought by a wealthy American widow who discovers the man's papers, which have been inadvertently left there.

She starts to go through them and finds that he was a Welshman called Havergal Wyllyams – a botanist who worked at Kew Gardens and wrote poetry in his spare time. He seems at first to have been an unremarkable and solitary man but as she goes through the papers a quite different story emerges, a story that will lead her in a botanical quest to Morocco, Patagonia and Madagascar and eventually to his birthplace in Wales, where she will meet the inspiration for much of Havergal's poetry.

It also becomes clear that perhaps his death was not as innocent as first thought.

This unusual and imaginative novel will entertain anyone who enjoys mystery, poetry, botany, global travel, Kew Gardens, conservation, Wales and the Welsh language – to name but a few of its many themes.